As a continual student of church growth, I [
for fresh ideas that will help me reach people. I consistently
return to my friend Charles Arn's work. His latest book, *Side
Door*, has sparked some new thoughts for me and will do the
same for anyone who is committed to reaching more people for
Jesus.

—NELSON SEARCY, lead pastor, The Journey Church,
New York; founder of ChurchLeaderInsights.com

The side door is a very useful approach that can help churches
become more missional. By using the natural relational pathways
of affinity that already exist among people, church leaders can
find new ways to serve and to grow the congregations they lead.
A well-articulated book.

—ALAN HIRSCH, author, activist, dreamer

Side Door is a must-read for missional practitioners who are
looking for relevant, need-meeting ways to connect incarnationally
with their communities by "entering into other people's worlds with
Christlikeness."

—MIKE SLAUGHTER, pastor, Ginghamsburg Church, Tipp City, Ohio

Those who desire to reach their community for the Lord will
love this book. *Side Door* contains great ways to extend ministry
into the community. This book empowers the imagination of
church leaders to think in nontraditional but very effective ways.
I will be recommending this book to all of my churches!

—STEPHEN F. BABBY, district superintendent,
Pacific Southwest District, The Wesleyan Church

Charles Arn's book on side door ministries is a terrific resource that helps church leaders and congregations unleash their creative imagination that will empower followers of Jesus to build new and genuine friendships with people.

—STANLEY DUECK, director, Transforming Practices,
Church of the Brethren

Charles Arn's *Side Door* is a much-needed resource for the church. He will help us think about ways to connect with people like Jesus did, to find out what others need, to spend enough time to understand their interests, to identify with them on their turf, and then, to introduce them to Christ.

—JIM DUNN, executive director, Church Multiplication
and Discipleship, The Wesleyan Church

Charles Arn's latest book is compelling! Charles not only provides an understanding and rationale for *Side Door*, but paints the picture, creates the vision, and provides a thorough, step-by-step handbook that helps us use members' passions and interests as a starting point for new ministries. His practical, hands-on approach, examples, and resources are invaluable in guiding churches to create and maximize new ministries that build relational bridges with those who don't yet know Jesus.

—SUE VON FANGE, minister for outreach and assimilation,
Trinity Lutheran Church, Clinton Township, Michigan

Side Door: How to Open Your Church to Reach More People offers the local church practical steps on how to become more faithful in fulfilling the Great Commission of Jesus Christ. This book provides an essential vision for churches to become missional and practical steps on how to get started today. *Side Door* is a crucial read for all our churches who are struggling with how to enable its members to have meaningful relationships with people outside the walls of the church.

—ERIC HOEY, director, Evangelism and Church Growth,
Presbyterian Mission Agency

No one, to my knowledge, knows more about helping local churches reach people for Christ than Charles Arn. With over three decades of experience in evangelism and church growth research, his insights are valuable and practical. *Side Door: How to Open Your Church to Reach More People* is needed by churches in the twenty-first century. Arn's insights and ideas will help churches obtain biblical church growth in the coming years.

—GARY L. MCINTOSH, professor of Christian ministry and leadership,
Talbot School of Theology, Biola University; author of *Here Today,
There Tomorrow: Unleashing Your Church's Potential* and
coauthor of *Being the Church in a Multi-Ethnic Community*

As our culture becomes more and more disenfranchised by scandal and division, the front door of the church becomes less attractive. But as Charles Arn clearly contends, it doesn't really matter what door is used as long as lost people find their way in. If you're looking for creative and effective ways to make connections with nonbelievers in your community, then read this book. A lot of authors tell us what we need to do. Charles details how we can do it!

—TOM MERCER, senior pastor, High Desert Church, Victorville,
California; author of *8 to 15: The World Is Smaller Than You Think*

Relationships are the key to effective evangelism but how and where people far from God connect to the church has been a mystery. The good news, as Dr. Arn points out, is that need- and interest-based side doors have the power to move people onto the pathway that leads to faith. Dr. Charles Arn not only shows how the church is actually growing, but teaches in a practical way how any church can create pathways through effective side door ministries. It's a must-read for all our leaders, and I would encourage you to read it and share it with your leaders. The good news is too good to remain inside the walls of our churches.

—BOB ORR, president, California State Christian University;
classic service pastor, Christ First Church, Covina, California

I was so excited about reading *Side Door*, and I could not put it down. I kept thinking of ways to apply it with my churches, and I cannot wait to share it with my pastors and leaders! This is such a complete manual on the step-by-step process of building side doors to reach the unreached.

—HERBERT PEÑA, evangelism director, West Coast Hispanic
Conference, International Pentecostal Holiness Church

In *Side Door*, Charles Arn refreshes many helpful church growth principles and strategically applies them for a newly emerging culture. Dr. Arn links the strengths of both missional and attractive models of ministry in what he calls, "incarnational evangelism." Anyone interested in a practical guide to help Christians "enter into other peoples worlds with Christlikeness" (Stott) will discover valuable insights in *Side Door*.

—DAVID SEBASTIAN, dean, Anderson University School of Theology

Side Door

Side Door

How to Open Your Church to Reach More People

CHARLES ARN
with Kwasi Kena

wesleyan
publishing
house

Indianapolis, Indiana

Copyright © 2013 by Charles Arn
Published by Wesleyan Publishing House
Indianapolis, Indiana 46250
Printed in the United States of America
ISBN: 978-0-89827-700-5
ISBN (e-book): 978-0-89827-701-2

Library of Congress Cataloging-in-Publication Data

Arn, Charles.
   Side door : how to open your church to reach more people / Charles Arn with
Kwasi I. Kena.
      pages cm.
   Includes bibliographical references.
   ISBN 978-0-89827-700-5 -- ISBN 978-0-89827-701-2 1. Church growth. I.
Kena, Kwasi Issa, 1957- II. Title.
   BV652.25.A76 2013
   253--dc23

                            2013030208

This book is revised from the previously published as *Heartbeat! How to Turn Passion into Ministry in Your Church.*

This book is dedicated to my son, Michael, whose creative approach to life reminds me of the kind of thinking required to build creative side doors in churches today.

Contents

Introduction   13

  1. Side Doors: What They Are —
     and Why They're So Important   23

  2. How Many Side Doors Do You Have?   41

  3. Do You Need Any More Side Doors?   57

  4. Getting Started on Your Side Door —
     Find the Passion   67

  5. How to Build a Side Door   81

  6. A Ministry Coach: Your Side Door Contractor   105

  7. Avoiding Problems with Your New Side Doors   121

  8. On Beyond Zebra   145

Epilogue   151

Appendix A: Side Door Assesment Chart   157

Appendix B: New Member Assessment Chart   159

Appendix C: Congregational Survey   161

Appendix D: Model Church Summary   167

Appendix E: Ministry Planning Chart   171

Appendix F: Goal Planning Worksheet   173

Appendix G: Publicity Planning Worksheet   175

Appendix H: Talking Points Discussion Guide   177

Notes   181

Reproducible resources are available for **FREE** online at
www.wphresources.com/sidedoor.

Introduction

Walking slowly to the podium, assisted by a cane and his research assistant, the theologian was met by a standing ovation from the overflow crowd at the Keswick Convention in England on the warm summer evening of July 17, 2007. Several years earlier, *Time* magazine had named him "one of the 100 most influential people on the planet." What would he say in this, his final public address, to those listening in that room and around the world?

John Stott began by recalling how perplexed he had been as a younger Christian about the answer to the question, "What is God's purpose for his people?" In his message that night, Stott described the resolution to his lifelong search: "I want to share with you where my mind has come to rest as I approach the end of my pilgrimage on earth and it is: God wants his people to become like Christ. Christlikeness is the will of God for the people of God."

Stott spent the rest of the evening addressing this matter of incarnational evangelism—a process, he noted, that can turn the world upside down. Stott's definition of incarnational evangelism was "entering into other people's worlds" with Christlikeness. Incarnational evangelism, said Stott, is the road the church must walk in the twenty-first century. Our evangelistic efforts often lead to failure, he observed, because we don't act like the Christ we proclaim. Quoting John Poulton, Stott noted, "The most effective preaching comes from those who embody the things they are saying. . . . What communicates now is basically personal authenticity. That is, Christlikeness."[1]

In two words, this is a book about *incarnational evangelism*. In it will be presented an effective, proven, yet enjoyable way for those in your church to enter into other people's worlds with contagious Christlikeness. Some call this the missional approach; others call it being externally focused. In its simplest form, incarnational evangelism is what the Christian life should be all about: becoming more like Christ in this world.

After this introduction, however, I would like to say good-bye to the term *incarnational evangelism*. That's because what I'll be sharing in this book is a process for laypeople—for those like me who aren't all that jazzed about big theological terms. Rather, we'll be using words like *side door* and *passion* and *friendship* and *fun*—words that more accurately describe the process we will be exploring.

This book is not so much about the what or why of incarnational evangelism as it is about the how. We'll be talking about how people can become great incarnational evangelists by riding motorcycles, searching for jobs, dealing with cancer, and dancing the hula. And we'll talk about how the people in your church can respond to Christ's command to "go and make disciples" while having the time of their lives.

Where Are We to Be Christlike?

A closer look at how Jesus' command to make disciples was given in the original Greek gives us insight into how he wants us to carry it out today. The word *go*, when Jesus said "go and make disciples" is more correctly translated "as you are going." In other words, Jesus was not telling the disciples to drop everything, pack their bags, and go off to a foreign land. He was saying, as you are going; as you are participating in your world; as you are involved in your normal, everyday encounters with people—in those contexts make disciples.

That is exactly the process of incarnational evangelism. And while Stott is right that incarnational evangelism has the power to turn the world upside down, incarnational evangelism also has the power to turn your church upside down—and your community in the process.

The encouraging news is that you don't have to be a megachurch to do it. While most megachurches are, in fact, practicing incarnational evangelism in the way we will talk about in this book, they don't have exclusive rights to the idea or a corner on the needs of people in our communities. Any church can respond to people as Christ did. There are hundreds of ways and places for the people in your church to become incarnational evangelists in your community. And in this book, I'll show you how. It's a process my friend, pastor Nelson Searcy, calls "putting wheels on the missional wagon."

The Silver Bullet for Making Disciples

A silver bullet is designed as "something that acts as a magical weapon; especially: one that instantly solves a long-standing problem." The term conveys the understanding that some new strategy, technology, or practice will solve a prevailing and undesirable condition. Based on more than thirty years of studying the process of evangelism and church growth, I can confidently say that there is a silver bullet for fulfilling Christ's command to go and make disciples. Here it is: The most effective evangelism, by far, occurs through meaningful relationships between Christians and non-Christians.

Did you know that more than twice as many people come to faith in Christ through relationships with Christian friends or relatives than all other reasons—combined?[2]

Many times in his ministry Jesus talked about and modeled this disciple-making silver bullet. To the man who had been demon-possessed, he said, "Go home to your family and tell them how much the Lord has done for you" (Mark 5:19). When Zacchaeus believed, Christ told him that salvation had come not only to him, but also to his friends and family as well (see Luke 19:9). After Jesus healed the son of a royal official, we learn that the official, with all his family and friends, believed (see John 4:53). In these events, Jesus was showing us that we are to share God's love with the people we already know "as we are going." This is the way the gospel travels.

In your next devotion time, look up the word *household* in your Bible concordance. You will find the term not only in the references above, but in many other verses as well. In the Greek, the word is *oikos*, and it has a fascinating meaning. The word *oikos* referred to those in a person's social network.[3] It included the person's immediate family (father, brother, wife, etc.). It included the person's extended family (cousin, brother-in-law, grandparent, nephew, etc.). *Oikos* referred to the servants who lived in first-century homes and likewise to the servants' families who lived there. The word also referred to the person's close friends, as well as work associates . . . no small number of people!

When the tremendous earthquake caused the Philippian jailer to desperately cry out, "What must I do to be saved?" Paul responded, "Believe in the Lord Jesus Christ, and you will be saved—you and your *oikos*" (Acts 16:31). Michael Green, British theologian and apologist, observes, "The early Christians knew that when the message of faith was heard and demonstrated by friends and family who were known and trusted . . . receptivity to the gospel increased tremendously."[4]

Existing relationships have been the primary means by which the gospel has traveled from the first-century church right up to today. One of the first books written by Donald McGavran, noted missiologist, was *Bridges of God*.[5] In it he explained how the gospel has timelessly crossed the bridges of established relationships between believer and unbeliever. Research still shows that it is through the naturally existing relationships of believers with nonbelievers that the gospel continues to spread most effectively.[6]

So incarnational evangelism is simply being intentionally Christlike in our normal, everyday lives—among the people in our social network.

A Problem with Shooting the Silver Bullet

But there is one essential requirement for being an incarnational evangelist: We must be close enough to unbelievers that they can observe and experience Christ in us. And there's the rub. The problem is that the longer people are in church, the more friends they have who are also in their church—and the fewer friends they have who are outside the church. Let me repeat this important problematic statement, because it is one of the major obstacles to the spread of the Christian gospel today: Most Christians have very few close friends who are non-Christian. Without such relationships, it is impossible for us to be Christlike. Remember Stott's definition of incarnational evangelism? "Entering into other people's worlds [with Christlikeness]." And he did not mean other Christians' worlds.

So how do we enter into a non-Christian's world to be Christlike if we don't really know any non-Christians? The answer is easy. We need to become more like Jesus—we need friends who are "tax collectors and sinners" (Matt. 11:19). Or, if you prefer Eugene Peterson's version, Jesus was spoken of as "a friend of the riffraff" (MSG).

The average new Christian can list twelve to thirteen non-believing friends and relatives in his or her social network.[7] But a curious thing begins to happen the longer people are Christians. Each year they can list fewer and fewer non-Christians in their social community. It's not that their friends and relatives have all become Christians, although this sometimes happens. Rather, it is a phenomenon that Donald McGavran calls "redemption and lift."[8] The more Christians learn about Christ and the more they want to become like Christ, the more comfortable they are around people who are on the same faith journey. Some longtime believers, in fact, have gotten to the point where they have no close friends or relatives outside the church.

One reason more than 85 percent of today's churches are not growing is that the social networks of people in these congregations are almost entirely within their four walls. Worse yet, most churches are actually programmed to encourage this relational isolation—church activities are geared toward existing members, successful church events are when a high percentage of members attend, small groups are formed primarily for those within the church. As a result, not only do church members have few non-Christian people with whom they associate, but non-Christians in the community have few or no close friends in the church.

From Christ's point of view, I believe, this is a serious problem. How can the church's missional task be accomplished if God's people are not in the world? "My prayer," said Jesus to his Father, "is not that you take them [Christ's followers] out of the world but that you protect them from the evil one" (John 17:15). In fact, Christians are supposed to be in the world, just not of the world.

Paul knew that he needed to connect with the "riffraff" before he could communicate with them: "I didn't take on their way of life. I kept my bearings in Christ—but I entered their world and tried to experience things from their point of view. I've become just about every sort of servant there is in my attempts to lead those I meet into a God-saved life. I did all this because of the Message. I didn't just want to talk about it; I wanted to be *in* on it!" (1 Cor. 9:21–23 MSG).

We are to be the salt of the earth (see Matt. 5:13). And salt does not season itself.

But like the Berlin Wall, which divided the German people and eventually created two separate cultures, there are walls today that isolate many Christians from non-Christians. We simply do not have doors in place that could allow people to pass through these "relational walls."

The Solution to the Problem

The solution is what this book is all about. It will help you and your church knock holes in those relational walls that separate your church from the people in your community. I call these holes *side doors*. As we will see, side doors are a proven and exciting way to build relationships with unchurched people. Side doors are a means of helping people inside your church to genuinely connect with people in your neighborhood. And side doors will allow people outside your church to experience real Christian community through contact with members of the body of Christ.

Sound impossible? Not only is it possible, it is happening! Such ministries "are the frontier topic for understanding the world's most effective churches," says noted missiologist George Hunter.[9] In this book, I want to share with you my research and experience about how to successfully build side doors. If I were introducing a brand new idea or program in these pages, I might be more concerned about whether I could make good on the promise of getting more people involved in more outreach while really enjoying it. But what is in this book are not new ideas, at least for the churches that are already implementing them.

You may be in a church that has plateaued or even declined in recent years. I believe that incarnational evangelism—as practiced through creating side doors—can be your key to effective new outreach and congregational growth.

Perhaps you are in the 15 percent of churches that are seeing growth in worship attendance. A side door building strategy will help you shift into overdrive and exponentially accelerate the number of people you reach in your community.

Perhaps you feel the "missional renaissance" that is going on in churches today has merit, and you want your congregation to become more missional in its focus and priorities. A side door building strategy is your answer to the question, "Where do we start?"

Well, actually, you have already started. And as you continue through this book, you will find a very helpful way to practice incarnational evangelism in your church. This step-by-step process comes out of having researched many churches that are doing it successfully. It comes from pilot projects in which I have tested this approach. And it comes from my observation that side doors are a proven way to knock holes in the walls that separate so many churches from so many people outside.

I really think you're going to enjoy this.

Side Doors

What They Are—and Why They're So Important

The prescription for growing a church is simple: more people must come in than go out. But realizing that positive flow of people is not quite as simple. In fact, more than eight out of ten Protestant churches in North America are not growing.

Having been a church consultant for more than thirty years, I have come to a sobering conclusion: The "front doors" of most churches are closing. Fewer people are visiting churches, and fewer visitors are staying. Put simply, there are hundreds of thousands of churches in America that have an insufficient number of visitors coming in their front doors to make up for those leaving through their back doors. As a result, churches that continue to rely on visitors as their primary source of growth will die within a few generations.

"Once upon a time, not so long ago," observes George Hunter, "churches relied on two 'front doors' for reaching people: the worship service and the Sunday school. Today, the most apostolic congregations reach even more people through 'side doors.'"[1]

Perhaps you have heard the term *side doors* applied to the church. It's not a new idea, and certainly not a complex one. But it is an increasingly critical idea for church leaders to understand. Side doors are a powerful way to harness the passion and energy in a church and to channel it into effective outreach. Side doors have the potential to help churches connect with—and reach—many new people in a community for Jesus Christ and his church.

What Are Side Doors?

I asked Reverend Todd Pridemore, minister of outreach at a medium-sized church in Columbia, Missouri, to tell about his church's side doors. Todd, along with a growing number of church leaders, is convinced that side doors can dramatically increase the number of people in a community who will be able to touch the face of Jesus. In these three short stories from Todd's church, you will see the exciting opportunities for ministry and outreach that side doors provide. You'll get the idea pretty quickly:

A couple of years ago, a woman in our congregation sensed a calling to invite a friend and the friend's family to church. However, this woman knew it was very unlikely that this unchurched family would respond to her invitation to attend the Sunday morning worship service. The member's children participated in an outreach-oriented basketball league at the church, so she invited her unchurched friend to enroll her two children in that activity as well. The kids got involved in the basketball program, and everyone loved the experience. Nearly two years later, the woman and her three children were baptized as new members of our church.

Another of our church members, a young father, met a new neighbor who did not attend any church in the community. The neighbor had moved into the area from another state and had virtually no friends nearby. Although the neighbor grew up as a Catholic, he did not consider religion and spirituality to be a significant part of his life. The church member took advantage of a fishing tournament sponsored by our church as a means of involving his new friend. After participating in two more fishing tournaments over the next four months, the neighbor began attending a Bible discussion group. He now attends our church regularly and is exploring Christianity in ways he never has before.

Still another church member, a young woman, had a coworker who had not gone to church since childhood. The member talked with her coworker about church and other religious issues, occasionally inviting her to attend some of the less-threatening activities at church, such as social events and women's activities. After months of being invited, the coworker finally attended a women's brunch at the church and enjoyed it immensely. After several more months of church-related conversations and invitations, the young lady finally attended a Sunday morning worship service. This woman felt God's presence through the worship service, as well as through the relationships she had developed with her coworker and others at the church. She felt compelled to investigate Christian faith on a deeper level, and she was recently baptized.[2]

These three stories focus on the lives of previously unchurched people who came into that church through some other means than its front door. Their first contact with Todd's congregation was not in the worship service or the Sunday school hour. In fact, Todd is convinced that had the front doors been the only way for people to get into his church, these people would likely not be involved there today. Instead, these people—and thousands of others in churches around the country—came to Christ and to the church through side doors.

So what exactly is a side door? A side door is a church-sponsored program, group, or activity in which a nonmember can become comfortably involved with the church on a regular basis. It is a group that provides an ongoing opportunity for a nonmember to develop meaningful and valued relationships with people in the congregation. The goal of an effective side door is to provide a place in which participants (both church members and nonmembers) can develop friendships around important things that they share in common.

Side doors cover the spectrum of human experience. They can be based on recreational pastimes or life events. They can be based on age, or they can span generations. But what binds the people in a side door group together is a passion they share for one particular thing, issue, or experience.

Sample Side Doors

Here are some examples of side doors. They are church-sponsored groups that have been started by and for people who:

- Ride motorcycles
- Have children in the military
- Own RVs
- Are recent widowers
- Are newlyweds
- Enjoy reading books
- Are unemployed
- Suffer from chronic pain
- Have husbands in jail
- Are nominal Jews
- Have spouses who are not believers
- Are fishermen
- Are single mothers
- Want to get in better physical condition
- Wish to help homeless families

- Play softball
- Are interested in end times
- Have a bed-ridden parent
- Are raising grandchildren
- Are moms with teenage daughters
- Need help managing their finances
- Enjoy scrapbooking
- Are children in blended families
- Have children with a learning disability
- Are married to men who travel frequently

- Enjoy radio-controlled airplanes
- Are pregnant
- Are affected by homosexuality
- Struggle with chemical dependency
- Are empty nesters
- Enjoy camping
- Are divorced and have no children
- Have a family member diagnosed with cancer
- Are single dads
- Enjoy SCUBA diving
- Are hearing impaired
- Ride mountain bikes

The idea of providing a place for unchurched people to connect with Christians before they become active Christ followers has actually been around for a while. John Wesley, the early religious pioneer, insisted on using side doors in his evangelistic ministry, as we read in the book *To Spread the Power*:

Wesley had three ultimate objectives for people: (1) that they experience the grace of God and the gift of faith, and become conscious followers of Jesus Christ; (2) that they be "united" with others in a "class" and a "society" [such as, be involved with a group of believers]; (3) that upon achievement of 1 and 2, they experience growth toward Christian perfection. It is crucial to point out that the first two objectives could be achieved in a person's life-history in either order, and the more usual sequence was, [two then one].

That is, most of the people who became Methodist converts first joined a class [a side door], and sometime later became conscious Christians! This helps to explain why Wesley, in his extensive open-air field preaching, never invited people to accept Jesus Christ and become Christians on the spot! That statement must surely shock those of us whose assumptions about public evangelism have been carved out in the Billy Graham era, as it would shock the evangelical Christians of any generation since Charles Grandison Finney first began inviting responders to what he called the "mourner's bench."[3]

Some two hundred fifty years after Wesley began the Methodist Church, Reverend Kwasi Kena, former director of evangelism ministries for the United Methodist Church, observed, "In order to proliferate, we must provide more 'side door' opportunities for entry into the life of our churches."[4]

So how does this play out in a local church? Motorcycles, for example, may be an interest of several young men in the church. Developing a church-sponsored side door ministry around motorcycles is a wonderful way to pursue a passion as well as to build friendships between members and nonmembers. In another church, a diagnoses of attention deficit hyperactivity disorder (ADHD) might lead several mothers to begin a ministry for parents who face a similar situation—a great possible side door for a church. A church-sponsored quilting club could grow out of the special interest of several women, while a ministry for divorced dads may emerge from the common experience of men in- and outside the church. While each of these interests is quite different from the others and ministries for these various people would obviously be different, the groups hold one characteristic in common. They bring people together—from in- and outside the church—who share a common passion. And when like-minded people come together around a common passion, deep friendships quickly sprout and grow. It is these new ministries, with their resulting relationships, that are side doors for many people to enter into the life and fellowship of the local church.

George Hunter analyzed the characteristics of what he called "apostolic churches" and observed that "one finds such churches reaching deaf people, and gambling addicts, and single-parent families, and people with mental illnesses, and Laotian immigrants—because a team of people within the church began following their hearts."[5]

As a trend, side doors are definitely on the way in. According to Lyle Schaller, a widely respected church consultant, most regular church attendees today who were born before 1935 made their initial contact with the church on Sunday morning through the front door. However, a large proportion of today's churchgoers who were born after 1935 made their initial contact through a side door.[6]

Gary McIntosh suggests that about 10 percent of the churches in the United States are side door churches in which "most of the new people who connect with the church made first contact through a ministry other than the worship service."[7] I have not tried to correlate Gary's 10 percent figure with the fact that only about 14 percent of the churches in America today are growing in worship attendance. But from my experience, I would not be surprised to find a high correlation between side door churches and growing churches. Reverend Craig Williford, recalling his experience in leading two growing, emerging churches, said,

"Our weekend services were very vital. But the side door ministries produced more evangelism and brought far more people into our church."[8]

Why Side Doors?

There are some good reasons why a strategy of building side doors will significantly enhance the ministry and outreach of your church.

More People Will Be Reached

The purpose of a side door is to provide a context where people who would not likely visit a church on their own can have a first-hand experience of God's love.

A popular topic of discussion these days is on the difference between "attractional" churches and "missional" churches. The attractional approach to outreach, which has been practiced in American churches for years, involves three basic steps: first, promote church events to "seekers"; then hope that visitors will attend those events; and finally, encourage the visitors to stay. The attractional approach can be an effective way to identify and connect with people who are interested in and receptive to spiritual things. However, as our culture becomes less and less Christian, fewer people are taking the initiative to attend church-sponsored events. More and more churches are finding that their front-door gains are insufficient to replace their back-door losses.

A new approach to outreach—the missional approach—is gaining influence as a means of helping non-Christian people encounter God's love. This type of outreach assumes that the people of God are called to intentionally demonstrate Christlikeness in their communities rather than to wait for their communities to come to church.[9] As more Christians are incarnational in their world, more people will experience, and be attracted to, the love of God.

Effective churches are actually practicing both attractional and missional outreach: "(a) They discover and invite all the people they can find who could be served through the church's present range of ministries; and (b) they develop new outreach ministries to serve and reach additional populations. Some churches now feature [fifty] or more lay-led outreach ministries, and they are unstoppable local movements."[10]

Side doors focus on the B in this list. Side door ministries help your church to become more missional by creating new outreach ministries that serve and reach additional people groups in your community. While front doors provide a way for people to come to your church, side doors provide a way for your church to go to people. Side doors are one of the best ways for us to "be [Christ's] witnesses . . . to the ends of the earth" (Acts 1:8).

More Kinds of People Will Be Reached

Churches tend to be rather homogenous. Most people in a particular church tend to look the same, sound the same, and talk the same. And for all practical purposes, their outreach potential is limited to others who look, sound, and talk the same as they do.

But when you begin creating new side doors into your church, not only will the number of your people connections grow, but the variety of your connections will grow as well. David Williamson, on staff at Saddleback Community Church, observes that "the more affinity and sub-affinity groups you have in your church, the more effective the church will be at reaching out to neighbors. Why? When you have groups for particular ages, languages, and other micro-communities, you increase the chance that people will find a group that fits them. Each affinity and sub-affinity group will reach different kinds of people."[11]

The variety of side door possibilities manifests itself in many ways: common interests, common marital status, life issues, family types, common dreams or passions, hobbies, or problems. When churches create new side doors, they often experience more growth than they had expected to. For instance, a church that begins a ministry for deaf people may find that it is also reaching the families of deaf people and many other people who are attracted to a church that cares enough to minister to people who are hearing impaired.[12] Several years from now, after creating a number of new side doors, you will look around your church and see people who represent a much greater diversity of age, marital and family status, culture, interests, concerns, and needs than you do now—most of whom came through your side doors.

More Members Will Be Involved

A survey by *Rev! Magazine* found the assumption that "20 percent of the people in church do 80 percent of the work" is optimistic; it's even fewer.[13] People do what they like to do. And if they find nothing that they like to do, they generally do nothing. Creating side doors based around people's existing interests, priorities, and passions eliminates the greatest volunteer recruiting obstacle—motivation. When people are already motivated, you don't need to worry about how to create it; you just need to channel it.

Below is a helpful continuum that illustrates why people do things.[14] As you look at it, ask yourself, "How do we motivate people in our church?" Many churches, unfortunately, tend toward the left end of the scale rather than toward the right.

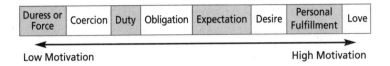

Duress or Force	Coercion	Duty	Obligation	Expectation	Desire	Personal Fulfillment	Love

← Low Motivation   High Motivation →

The common approach to involving church members in ministry is for leaders to promote an "institutional" agenda (toward the left side of this scale). In such churches, members are encouraged to "join this group," "volunteer for that program," and "attend those meetings." This approach to lay ministry seeks to direct members to the church programs that leaders think are important.

In contrast are the (fewer) churches where leaders promote an "individual" agenda (toward the right side of the scale). Here, more emphasis is placed on encouraging members to create or become involved in ministries related to their existing interests. For example, a woman at Frazer United Methodist Church in Montgomery, Alabama, learned that when premature babies were born in Montgomery's several hospitals, the hospital and the parents often could not find clothing for a three-pound baby; apparently no clothing manufacturer serves that small market. So the church encouraged the woman to organize a group of women who love to sew. The group (made up of church members and nonmembers) now sews the booties, gowns, and caps for every premature baby born in any hospital in Montgomery. They take the clothing to the hospitals, and they minister to anxious families. While the ministry has no strings attached, many families of preemies have joined Frazer Church, some as new Christians.[15]

More Members Will Be Involved in Outreach

Simply having more people involved in church activities is no guarantee that more people will be reached for Christ. *What* they are doing is at least as important as *whether* they are doing.

Donald McGavran, in his significant work *Understanding Church Growth*,[16] provides a helpful way for churches to evaluate the strategic deployment of laypersons into ministry. He categorizes potential leaders into "classes." The two most important, for our purposes, are Class I and Class II. Class I leaders are those whose time and energy focus on maintaining the existing church. They serve as deacons, teachers, ushers, greeters, choir members, elders, etc. As McGavran says, "They are good people. They are God's people. The church would be a poor place without them. But there is very little direct relationship between Class I activities and the actual growth of the church."[17]

Class II workers are those whose time and energy focus outward, beyond the walls of the church. They interact with people who are not part of the church and build connections with people in the community. They follow-up with visitors. They welcome new neighbors to the community. They represent their church in public events. The relationship between Class II roles and church growth is direct and causal.

The typical non-growing church has a Class I to Class II ratio of approximately ninety-five to five. That is, for every one hundred people involved in some sort of church ministry, 95 percent of them are in Class I (maintenance) roles, while only 5 percent are in Class II (outreach) roles. The good news is that building new side doors will increase the number and percent of people in your church who are involved in Class II activities. And that will increase conversion growth.

More Groups Will Be Started

Here's an equation that is crucial to a church's vitality: new groups equals new growth. In fact, I suggest a new-group ratio of one to five. This means that if you want to increase the percentage of your church members who are involved in small groups, you will need to start new groups, with one of every five groups being less than two years old.[18]

Why is there a direct relationship between new groups and new growth? Because every group has a saturation point. Like a sponge that cannot hold any more water, groups get to a point at which they cannot hold any more members. I have found that approximately 90 percent of all groups saturate after two years. Beyond this point in time, it becomes extremely difficult for newcomers to break in. Relationships have developed among the existing members, experiences have been shared, trust has been deepened, and the sense of community has grown. It's a wonderful place to be if you're on the inside, but it's very hard to get in if you're on the outside. This is not intentional exclusion, but it does happen. And it's real.

The secret for dealing with this normal phenomenon of group saturation is easy: start new groups. New side door groups are easy to start because they bring people together around meaningful common interests. And the bonding that occurs in these new groups creates the same wonderful experience that we just described—relationships are strengthened among the members, experiences are shared, trust is deepened, and the group becomes a meaningful community.

More Members Will Invite Friends

Churches grow when friends bring friends. The antithesis is also true: Churches don't grow when friends don't bring friends.

"[Our church] provides numerous 'side door' ministries that give members the opportunity to bring friends into contact with the church family," says the website of Center Grove Presbyterian Church in Edwardsville, Illinois. With more than a dozen side doors already running, the church says, "Additional side door ministries and activities are added as the Lord raises up members with the calling and commitment to implement and lead them."[19]

The typical church member will more likely invite a friend to a side door activity than he or she will invite that same friend to a Sunday morning service. However, a fascinating thing happens when the friend begins participating in a side door group: The person makes other friends in that group, many of whom attend the church. Then, when a special church activity or Sunday service is planned, the chances are excellent that the nonmember will be invited to the event, and the nonmember will attend with friends from the group. Remember Todd Pridemore's three stories in which he shared how this exact pattern unfolded in his church?

More New Members Will Stay

Most pastors know the unfortunate reality that not all new members become active members. Why do some leave while others stay? Lyle Schaller tells us, "Among those not related by kinship to a congregation, those most likely to become active members are those who become part of a group, and develop meaningful relationships with others in that group, *before* formally uniting with that congregation. They are assimilated before they join."[20]

That is exactly why churches whose new members come through a side door have higher assimilation rates—those new people developed meaningful relationships with others in the church and found a sense of belonging, acceptance, and value in their side door group *before* they joined. In fact, it is not unusual for persons in the group to become "assimilated" even before they become believers. Social connectedness can (and often should) precede theological conversion. "We don't worry about people dropping out of church who are connected to a small group," says Rick Warren, pastor of a church with over fifteen thousand members. "We know that those people have been effectively assimilated."[21]

Your Church's Community Visibility Will Increase

Churches with high public exposure (at least the good kind) tend to have a higher percentage of walk-in visitors. So what gives a church high public exposure? The media. And how does a church get media exposure? By doing something newsworthy.

Many side door groups and activities, particularly ones focused on issues of contemporary interest, are newsworthy. Local newspapers and television stations will often feature church activities that positively affect the local community. Some years ago, for example, Fourth Presbyterian Church in Chicago purchased property in the infamous Cabrini-Green community. They decided to transform the Chicago Avenue site into a cooperative garden as a way to develop relationships with the families in the area, and in 2010 the garden became an urban farm as the church partnered with another ministry to expand its growth.[22] This side door for building relationships received much media coverage and increased visitor traffic to the church as a result. People-helping-people ministries get noticed. And many side doors are just that.

Dependency on Your Facility Will Decrease

If your church building is more than twenty-five years old, chances are good that the building is negatively affecting your growth. Church buildings can be growth-restricting obstacles.[23] It's a bad sign when a visitor walks into your facility and the architecture alone makes him or her feel uncomfortable. Side door groups don't have to (and sometimes shouldn't) meet in the church facility. Rather, people connections can happen in the community—in the real world.

You Will Change from a Single-Cell Church to a Multi-Cell Church

Half the churches in the United States have under eighty people in attendance. These churches are called single-cell churches, and at that size, they are confronting the most difficult barrier for any church to break through.

A single-cell church is one in which community, fellowship, caring, and spiritual growth occur when the entire congregation is together. Sociologically, a church cannot grow beyond one hundred people (the approximate limit of a single-cell church) without newcomers encountering an unyielding sociological wall.

But when the sense of community, fellowship, caring, and spiritual growth begins to occur in the smaller units of the church— when the church begins to move from a single-cell organism to a multi-cell organism—its potential for growth increases dramatically. Side door groups are tailor-made to facilitate a church's metamorphosis from single-cell to multi-cell.

Your Church Will Not Be Dependent on Walk-In Visitors

In chapter 3, I will show you how to determine whether you have enough Sunday visitors to grow. But as I have already noted, most churches don't. Nonmembers who become part of a side door group, however, develop friendships with people in your church. And those new friendships with church members greatly increase the likelihood of their visiting other church-related events and becoming part of your faith community. Side doors increase visitor flow.

Let me encourage you to seriously consider the power of side doors, regardless of your church's size, shape, or color. Big churches can have side doors. Little churches can have side doors. Urban, rural, and suburban churches can have side doors, as can growing churches or declining ones. Any church that desires to be more intentional and more effective in outreach will find side doors to be vital and strategic.

The Risks

Obviously, there are many good reasons to consider building new side doors to connect your church with your community. "The best churches and denominations encourage new ministries," says Don Cousins.[24]

But you may be wondering about the potential risks in committing to a strategy of side doors. And there are some. Let me briefly give you three.

First, a commitment to building side doors will create more connections to unchurched people than you have probably had for some time. The results of these new relationships may not always be comfortable to members who have a "church is for us" mentality.

Second, a commitment to building side doors will mean that some of your members now involved in Class I (institutional maintenance) roles will be attracted to Class II (community outreach) activities. The results of these time and personnel recommitments may not always be comfortable to members who have a "church is for us" mentality.

Third, a commitment to building side doors will mean that members who are involved in beginning these new ministries will need more freedom and flexibility than your church may be used to giving members who are not in elected positions of authority. The results of this new freedom may not always be comfortable to members who have a "church is for us" mentality.

After it's all said and done, however, if you were to ask Jesus what his priorities are for your church, he would probably respond the same way he did to the demon-possessed man whom he had just healed: "Go home to your [*oikos*] and tell them how much the Lord has done for you" (Mark 5:19).

The simple rule is this: The more "doors" you provide into your church, the more unbelievers in your community will walk through them and discover the amazing and fulfilling life God has in store for them.

How Many Side Doors Do You Have?

Aren't most church groups and activities side doors, or at least potential side doors? After all, visitors are always welcome at, and often invited to, most church functions. So what really is a side door, and what is it not?

Remember high-school chemistry and those little pieces of litmus paper—the blue paper turned red in the presence of acid, and the red turned blue in a base solution? Well, there is a litmus test for side doors. In this chapter, we will examine eight ingredients for an effective side door. Each of them must exist for an activity to be considered a legitimate side door. If all these ingredients are not present, the activity may still be a helpful and important part of your church, but it is not a side door, and it will not increase your outreach in the same measure as a genuine side door. An important goal of later chapters in this book will be to help you build each of these ingredients into your side doors. But for now, here's the test.

1. Side Doors Involve Members and Nonmembers

This first ingredient is the most important. Side doors must involve people from both in- and outside the church. The word *involve* is key. It does not simply mean that an activity is open to outsiders. Nearly everything we do in the church is open to outsiders. Rather, a genuine side door activity is planned, programmed, and evaluated around the assumption that church attendees and non-attendees will both be present.

After a side door activity is concluded, one of the first evaluative questions should be: How many unchurched people were there? If the answer is none, the discouragement should be as great as if the same answer had been given to the question: How many people were there? In other words, if there are no contacts or connections with unchurched people at a side door activity, the event is a failure, no matter how many church members are there.

Donald McGavran, one of the most respected missiologists of the twentieth century, was once asked, "Can small groups help the church grow?" He responded, "Small groups do promote friendship, love, harmony, mutual support. All those things are desirable. However, if the small group consists exclusively of people who are already Christians, exclusively of the existing members of the church, then it has very little meaning for the growth of the church. On the other hand, if the small group makes it a point to include within itself those who have not accepted Christ, then the small group is one of the most effective ways of winning people to Christ."[1]

Based on my observations of successful side doors I suggest a churched-to-unchurched ratio in your side door activities of at least seventy-five to twenty-five. That is, no more than 75 percent of a side door group should be represented by members of your church, and at least 25 percent should be nonmembers. A better ratio is sixty-six to thirty-four. An ideal ratio is fifty to fifty.

When evaluating your church groups and activities, use the following continuum to determine whether or not they are side doors.

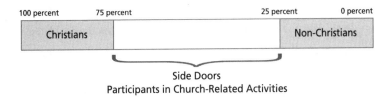

Side Doors
Participants in Church-Related Activities

Many church activities are populated mostly by Christians and church attendees: Sunday school and adult Bible classes, small-group meetings, men's and women's fellowships, and church dinners. These are all nice events, but they're not really side doors, since they are not a major source of new connections with new people.

On the other end of the continuum, some churches mistakenly believe that local community groups who use their facilities are side doors. For example, I once saw the following quote on the website of a church in southern Minnesota: "Our side door ministries are various groups from the surrounding community that use our facility and provide opportunities for us to serve their needs: Chinese Day Care, Over-Eaters Anonymous, Alcoholics Anonymous, Clutterers Anonymous, Red Cross Blood Mobile, Home School Writing Project, Bonsai Society, Scottish Dancers, and Lions Club."

It is nice that this church makes their facilities available. And certainly the topics of these gatherings are the kind of special interests that could make exceptional side doors. But when I followed up on this church, I found that these groups were simply using the church's facilities and were making no contribution to the growth of that church.

Can an existing group in your church *become* a side door? It's difficult. When a group of people has been together for years, it is very hard for a significant number of newcomers to become involved in that group, especially if they are unchurched newcomers. In chapter 1, I spoke of a group's saturation point: approximately 50 percent of all groups stop growing after one year, 90 percent after two years. Certainly it is possible, and of course desirable, for existing groups to invite newcomers. And any group should be happy to receive new members. But side doors should have a significant number (at least 25 percent) of unchurched people involved in the group from the outset. Rather than trying to force existing groups to become side doors, it is far better to begin a new group or activity that is designed to be a side door ministry from the start.

As we go through the subsequent characteristics of side doors, you will find that many of the groups in your church meet the remaining criteria. That is why this first ingredient is so critical— at least 25 percent of the group should be unchurched.

2. Side Doors Bring People Together Who Have Important Things in Common

There are several key ideas in this sentence, the obvious one being "things in common." We all gravitate toward those with whom we share common interests. Think about your friends. Chances are that you have a number of things in common with them. Affinity provides us with things to talk about together, places to go together, and experiences to share together. Marriage counselors tell us that the more things a couple has in common, the more likely it is that they will be friends, enjoy their time together, and develop a strong, lifelong relationship. "People connect most naturally with others who are like them," observed the pastor of a church that thrives around side door ministries. "Common interests, ideas, studies, practices, hardships . . . these make the best framework for relational connectivity."[2] Effective side doors involve people who share things in common—and the more things they have in common, the better.

Another key word in this criterion for a side door is *important.* Ask people how they would define themselves and listen to them describe the important things in their life. Some of these things they have consciously chosen, such as a career, a hobby, or a place to live. Other definers, however, may be beyond their control: having a child with Down syndrome, being unemployed, or navigating single parenthood. Some of the important things about us are positive and pleasurable; others are not. But they define who we are. And when we are with others who share similar important things in their lives, we connect. As C. S. Lewis so insightfully wrote, "Friendship is born at that moment when one person says to another: 'What! You, too? I thought I was the only one.'"[3]

Things that are important to people will likely fall into one or more of the following categories:

- Age
- Marital status
- Family status
- Interests or hobbies
- Needs, concerns, or problems
- Religious background or attitude
- Cultural or ethnic identity

In my research on church side doors, I have found that most side door ministries can be grouped into one of two general categories: recreational or support. But within these two areas, the interests and passions found among the people in a church are almost endless. For example, the Rhema Bible Church near Tulsa, Oklahoma, has a variety of recreational side doors they call LINK groups (Loving, Involving, Nurturing, Keeping). Each of their groups grew out of the passion of someone in the church (see below).

Rhema Bible Church LINK Groups

- Aviation (for licensed pilots to connect)
- Rhema Tread (running)
- Entrepreneur (a network of entrepreneurs already in business ventures)
- Polynesian (ethnic group meets once a month)
- Knitting and Crocheting (for those who do these activities or want to learn)
- Military (those with military interests share stories and food together)
- Glory Riders (rev up your motorcycles for joy rides and special events)
- Sharps and Flats (musicians, songwriters, and singers develop their talents)
- Must Like Dogs (activities involving dogs)
- Photography (enjoy learning masterful techniques)
- Gardening (green thumbs share gardening advice on flowers and veggies)
- Quilting and Sewing (work on projects and share fellowship)
- Paintball (team building, competitive, fun, family!)
- Day Trekkers (day-long hiking trips once a month)
- Scrapbook Junkies (enthusiasts have fun sharing their hobby together)
- Music Composers (musicians, singers, song writers, and worship leaders develop their talents and conduct ministry outreach)
- Mississippi (for anyone who loves the state!)
- Second Sunday Lunch Bunch (this fun group promotes socialization among all ages)
- Writer's Bloc (those with a passion for the written word develop their skills and enjoy writing opportunities)

Rather than recreational side doors, NorthRidge Church in Plymouth, Michigan, focuses their side doors on providing support through life's tough times. They call their side doors LifeShare groups. (See the box below for a list of their side doors specifically for women; the church has other side doors for men and families.)

NorthRidge Church Women's LifeShare Groups

- Boundaries (when to say yes and how to say no)
- Changes That Heal (for women who have been or are in unhealthy relationships)
- Chronic Pain and Illness (Why am I going through this?)
- Overcoming Depression and Anxiety (studies and discusses the book *Learning to Tell Myself the Truth*)
- Divorce Care (for hurting people experiencing the pain of separation)
- Domestic Abuse (there is hope through understanding the root of anger and abuse; studies the book *Why Does He Do That?*)
- Family Group (for a family member or concerned friend of an alcoholic)
- First Place (transform your life with the Bible's way to weight loss)
- GriefShare (to help those who are grieving the death of a loved one)
- Hopeful Hearts (a support group for couples or individuals dealing with infertility)
- Twelve Steps to Freedom (for those who realize that alcohol or drugs are interfering with normal living)
- Partner Care (learn how God loves addicted people differently and effectively)
- Shout! (a Christ-centered group for women in recovery from past physical and/or sexual abuse)
- Living Beyond Trauma (for individuals and/or families who have experienced trauma through military duty, their police or fireman occupation, work as an EMT and/or as medical personnel, or as victims of violent crime)

Both of these churches intentionally use their groups to connect with unchurched people in their community. Side doors bring together people who share one or more things in common.

3. Side Doors Intentionally Build Relationships

An important question to ask about intended side doors is this: Will they be places where people can become real friends? Effective side doors are places in which meaningful friendships don't just happen; they are planned. Side doors are relational greenhouses in which the seeds of friendships are planted, nurtured, watered, and grown. People in a side door group play together, laugh together, and cry together. As friendships grow, participants often spend time beyond the group's scheduled activities simply sharing life together.

When people first begin attending a side door activity, they come because the topic of the group is of interest to them. But over multiple gatherings, an effective side door leader will intentionally nurture relationships among participants. The graph below illustrates an ideal change in what group members come to value as they are involved in their side door activity.

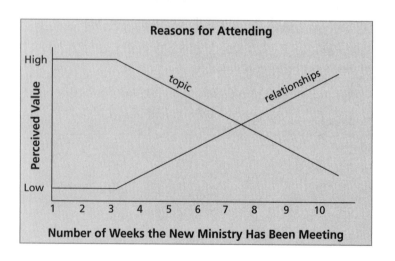

In the first few weeks, people attend a new class, group, club, or activity because they are attracted to a particular topic or a specific experience. But as participants get to know each other and feel more and more comfortable together, the seeds of friendship begin to grow. At some point, if the leader plans time for nurturing new friendships, the perceived value of the relationships actually surpasses the value of the content or nature of activity.

I have found that about 75 percent of the time, when such groups reach the end of their planned study or activity, members want to continue meeting. Why? Because they have come to value their relationships in and of themselves. The topic—the initial reason for their gathering—has become almost incidental. And that's a healthy evolution—from a collection of people to the birth of a group.

For this relational metamorphosis to occur, a group should meet *at least* six times over a six-month period. Of course, some side door gatherings will meet weekly for years, and that's great. But a minimum of six meetings allows people to get to know each other, remember names, and start building history through common experiences. (We will explore more about how to build such community later in the book.)

4. Side Doors Meet Deeper Human Needs

One of the saddest things about a non-Christian's life is that he or she does not experience the joy, comfort, and peace that a relationship with God could provide. While a side door gathering need not be overtly spiritual, its participants should get a taste of how God's love can speak to their deeper needs through the love of God's people. What are these deeper human needs that, when met, will give nonbelievers a firsthand taste of glory divine? People are looking for:

- Connection and community as they feel increasingly disconnected and isolated in their world;
- A sense of balance in a busy and stressful life;
- Authentic relationships amid their many shallow, superficial encounters;
- Spiritual answers as work, material possessions, and entertainment fail to meet their unfilled hunger; and
- Help through transitions as the pace of change in their life increases.

When unchurched people begin to feel a sense of hope that such needs can possibly be met in a church-related group, it provides a powerful attraction to the source of that hope. For example, suppose you are not a church attendee but have been involved in a hiking group sponsored by a nearby church. Some months into your involvement with the group, your spouse goes into the hospital for surgery. The members of your hiking group bring dinners over for you. They pick up your third-grade child from school in the afternoons. They pray for your spouse before their hikes and regularly ask about his or her condition. As your spouse improves, they thank God for answered prayer. What effect do you think such caring acts will have on you, your spouse, and your family?

In a word, I call this *love*. The function of a healthy side door group is to provide a place in which people outside the Christian faith can begin to experience God's love through God's people. When one or more of a person's deeper needs are met, Stanley

Mooneyham's words ring true: "Love spoken can be easily turned aside. Love demonstrated is irresistible."[4] (Again, we'll learn how to see this happen in your side doors later in the book.)

5. Side Doors Require the Involvement of a Local Church

Architecturally speaking, a side door must be part of some kind of structure. I have never seen a side door standing alone in the middle of a field. Spiritually speaking, the same principle applies. Side doors cannot exist apart from the ministry of a local church. They are not intended as a forum for doing good works for needy people as an end in itself. They are not designed to help people make a faith commitment without drawing them to a faith community. Side doors connect people in a church with people in the community with the goal of forming relationships that *bring those people into the body of Christ*. Believers are called to be a part of Christ's body as arms, legs, hands, and feet. Side doors are built to reach lost people for Jesus Christ and to add to the church daily those who are being saved (see Acts 2:47).

In this respect, I worry about how the currently popular "missional movement" can sometimes result in people devaluing the local church. As an instructor at Wesley Seminary in Marion, Indiana, I teach a class called The Missional Church. I have observed that many students, after reading books by missional authors and watching videos of missional teachers, will sometimes throw out the baby with the bathwater. That is, they conclude that the ultimate goal of a missional church is to go into the community to do good works in the name of Christ and to expand the kingdom of God. Whether the needy folks in the community ever come to faith and membership in a local church seems to lose its preeminence and is certainly not a criterion for defining success in the missional agenda.

For example, a missionally inclined blogger recently lit into Andy Stanley's five-million-dollar bridge. North Point Community Church, a congregation known for its commitment to outreach and evangelism, had grown to the point at which parking had become problematic. Stanley told his parishioners of the church's need to ease traffic congestion by constructing a bridge off the main thoroughfare into the church. His letter included the following paragraph: "Is it [the bridge] worth it? It all depends. If our mission is to be a church that's perfectly designed for the people who already attend, then we don't need a bridge. But if we want to continue to be a church unchurched people love to attend, then yes, it's worth it. . . . I believe creating a second access point allows us to stay on mission."[5]

It seems obvious that Stanley's commitment as a pastor is to make disciples and to involve them in the local church. But the missional blogger responds, "This makes me sick. This is completely un-missional. Missional churches are not attractional churches. Missional churches send out their parishioners as missionaries to the world, not bring them to church over a five-million-dollar edifice to speed up their exit and entry."[6]

In their zeal to create the kingdom of God in the world, some who buy into the missional movement seem to have (or develop) a bias against the established church. Their commitment is to bring the kingdom of God into the community. But the success of those kingdom-expanding efforts does not seem to be evaluated on whether those who are exposed to the kingdom are ever reached and assimilated into active membership and participation in a local church.

A commitment to side doors, however, demands a high view of the church—a recognition that the church is absolutely essential. It is not *a* body of Christ; it is *the* body of Christ. Not just a bride, but the bride of Christ. The church is held to be the central part of God's plan for the salvation and discipling of people and nations. New converts must not only believe in Jesus Christ, but must become responsible members of the church. If the Bible is to be taken seriously, we cannot hold any other point of view. Becoming a Christian means becoming a part of the body. In fact, unless the non-Christians we reach out to believe in Christ and become part of the church—personified through a local congregation—the ultimate value of our activities must be questioned. This is the high view of the church. A low view of the church, on the other hand, is that whether or not you belong to the church is a matter of choice. If you like it, you can belong; if you don't, you don't have to.

Side doors lead people into the Christian faith and community through the local church.

6. Side Doors Are Managed and Initiated by Laypeople

A few years ago, I was part of a study in which we asked pastors, "What is the most frustrating aspect of your ministry?" The number one response, regardless of denomination or theology, was, "Getting people in the church to participate in the work of the church."

The good news is that side doors provide people with the opportunity to start and participate in an activity of personal interest while positively affecting the life and growth of their church. When this happens, the pastor's problem of motivating people ceases to be a problem because side door activities tap into motivation that members already have. People don't have to be motivated by a pastor; they are already motivated by their passion.

The bad news for some pastors, however, is that side doors mean a loss of control. Rick Warren, whose church puts a strong emphasis on plugging members' passions into side door ministries, has observed, "If you want your church to be a place where all sorts of talents and abilities are expressed in a creative way that draws people to Christ, you have to give up control and trust people with ministry."[7] A church that wants to create side doors simply needs to identify the passions that already exist in the congregation and then *channel* them. In chapter 4, we will look at how to identify those passions that could become side door ministries.

7. Side Doors Begin a Disciple-Making Process

Most new Christians who become active church members have heard the gospel more than once, from more than one source. In fact, one study found that those who became vital, growing Christians had heard the gospel presented an average of six times before they made their commitment to Christ. This was in contrast to those who made a decision but never became integrated into a church: on average, they heard the gospel only twice.[8] Being exposed to Christian faith multiple times, through multiple people and programs, provides non-Christians a more complete picture of what it means to be a Christ follower.

The application? Side door events should not be the only place an unchurched person encounters God. While a side door group will often be the first extended contact that an unchurched person has with Christian people, it should not be the last. The new friendships made in a side door group or activity provide a natural context for nonmembers to be invited to other Christ-related events.

A nonmember on your church softball team, for example, could be invited by a friend to the Christmas Eve service, a special concert, or a church-sponsored beach or mountain trip. Inviting the friend's family to the church's Easter egg hunt or a camping trip would be natural and appropriate. An invitation to attend a worship service may certainly be extended at some point, although it would probably be most appropriate as the fifth or sixth contact rather than the second or third. The more times a person is exposed to Christianity, the better he or she understands the implications of the Christian life and faith. In other words, a side door is not an isolated entry event, but the first step on an extended "entry path" into the church.

8. Side Doors Make the Benefit Worth the Cost

We all have places to go, people to see, and things to do. That's life. But the choices we make about where we go, whom we see, and what we do are based on our assessment of its benefit versus its cost. A side door group will prosper as participants tell their friends of its value. Therefore, in planning an effective side door (which we will see how to do in chapter 5), we must realize that prospective participants will be asking, "Is the benefit of participating in this activity worth the cost?" Prince of Peace Lutheran Church in Burnsville, Minnesota, has it right. Whenever they consider starting a new side door group, they ask prospective attendees, "What kind of group would you change your schedule to attend?"[9]

Suppose, for example, you are interested in developing a healthier lifestyle. With the encouragement of your church, you are excited at the prospect of beginning your own women's fitness group (assuming you're a woman). Would you find such a focus to be boring? Would you dread the meetings and count the seconds until they were over? Of course not. You would love planning and participating in the group. You would meet women who share your passion. You would make new friends. And what about those women in your group who might not initially attend your church but were committed to the goal of physical fitness? The health-related information they would receive, the exercises they would do, the encouragement they would give and receive, the friends they would make—those benefits would far outweigh their costs.

The genius of side door ministries, as you will discover in your own church, is that people enjoy being part of them. Members love them. nonmembers love them too, because people love to do what they love to do—especially with others who love to do it too. And the new relationships that develop around those passions are cherished for years.

Do You Need Any More Side Doors?

Would your church benefit from adding some (more) side doors? Let's discuss six self-diagnostic questions and measures to help you decide.

Do You Have Enough Visitors to Grow?

The answer to this question depends on your visitor volume. Visitor volume is the percentage of newcomers (prospective members) who attend your church-related events. If you have a visitor volume of 5 percent or greater, you probably don't need any more side doors.

Calculating your visitor volume is not difficult. To do so, first determine the total number of visitors who attended any of your church-related events in the past fifty-two weeks, including, but not limited to, weekend services. For instance, if a couple visited a worship service and a Christmas Eve service, count that as four (one service per person). If one person visited a worship service three times in the past year, count that as three. Count first-, second-, and third-time visitors (not just first-timers). Do not include visitors from out of town, and only count those thirteen years old or older.

Next, add the total number of participants who attended these same events; include church members *and* visitors.

Finally, divide the total number of participants by the total number of visitors. This will give you your visitor volume—the average percentage of visitors per event for the past twelve months. (For example, if a church's total annual visitor count was 253, and its total annual attendance at those events was 9,149, then its visitor volume would be 2.8 percent.) It will be even more helpful to calculate your visitor volume for the prior two years, and then compare all three years in order to look for trends.

Now back to the question: Did you have enough visitors in your church last year to grow? If your visitor volume was 5 percent or greater, you probably have enough visitors. (Although not every church with a visitor volume of 5 percent or higher experiences growth, since there are other factors we will consider below.) If your visitor volume is significantly less than 5 percent, however, you need more side doors, since the answer to the initial question is most likely, "No."

Do You Keep Enough Visitors to Grow?

The answer to this question depends on your visitor retention. Visitor retention is the percentage of visitors who became involved in your church within a year of their first visit. These visitors may not yet be members, but they now regularly attend one or more of your church's activities. If you have a visitor retention of more than 20 percent, you probably do not need any more side doors.

To calculate your visitor retention rate, list the name of each person who has visited at least one church event in the past two to eighteen months. Then determine whether that person is now a regular attendee. Below is a simple chart to help determine your visitor retention rate. (You can easily recreate this chart on your own, adding enough lines for each visitor.)

Name of visitor	Date of first visit (within the past two to eighteen months)	Now regularly attending? (yes or no)

Once you have completed the chart, simply add the number of yeses in the right column and divide the total number of visitors on the chart by the number of yeses. The result will be your visitor retention rate. For example, if a church had seventy-nine people who visited a church event for the first time during the past two to eighteen months, and twenty-one of those people are now active, the church's visitor retention rate would be 26.5 percent.

A healthy visitor retention rate is 20 percent or higher. That is, if your church keeps at least one out of every five visitors, you are doing well. If your visitor retention rate is less than 20 percent, you should consider building some new side doors.

How Many of Your Present Activities Are Side Doors?

To answer this question, duplicate the Side Door Assessment Chart (appendix A) and add enough rows to list every church-sponsored activity that meets at least monthly.

In the first column, list all church activities. This includes youth events, children's and adult classes, small groups, support groups, choir practices, sports events, and the like. Do not include your worship services, since those are front doors. Also, do not include church board or committee meetings, since those are closed doors. Finally, do not include activities hosted by organizations that use your facilities but are not sponsored by your church, since those are not doors at all.

In the second column, calculate the average attendance for each meeting during the past six months. (Total the number of people who were at each meeting, then divide that total by the number of meetings.)

In the third column, record the average number of unchurched people in these meetings. (Add the total number of unchurched people who were at each meeting, then divide that total by the number of meetings.)

In the fourth column, calculate the percentage of unchurched people who participated in each activity. (Divide the second column by the third column and then multiply the answer by one hundred to get a percentage.)

In the fifth column, determine which of the groups are functioning as side doors. If the fourth column is between 25 percent and 75 percent, your group is functioning as a side door. If it is less than 25 percent or more than 75 percent, indicate that it is not a side door.

Finally, calculate the totals at the bottom of the chart.

A good rule of thumb is that at least 20 percent of your existing church activities (classes, small groups, monthly socials, youth gatherings, men's and women's groups, etc.) should be side doors. If your number is lower, consider creating some new side doors.

How Many of Your New Members/Attendees Were Previously Unchurched?

People come into a church by one of three ways: biological growth, transfer growth, or conversion growth. Biological growth takes place when children of existing Christians become active in the church. Transfer growth occurs when Christians transfer their membership from one church to another. Conversion growth occurs when people commit or rededicate their lives to Christ and then affiliate with a church. I have noticed that what is often perceived by some to be significant church growth turns out to be primarily transfer growth—congregational musical chairs. Conversion growth, of course, is what Christ was talking about when he said, "Go and make disciples" (Matt. 28:19). In a healthy church, at least 20 percent of the newcomers are both new to that local church and also new to the kingdom.

Complete the New Member Assessment Chart in appendix B to help you consider the source of your newcomers. If possible, include information from the past five years. If your average conversion growth rate is less than 20 percent of your total growth, you need more side doors. If your rate is between 20 percent and 40 percent, your church is healthy. If it is more than 40 percent, and your church is over ten years old, write a book. (Most new churches typically have a conversion rate of more than 50 percent, but within ten years that percentage often declines.) Regardless of your conversion rate, if you regularly start side doors, you will increase the number of unchurched people with whom you have contact, many of whom will move from outside Christ's family to inside.

What Is Your Church's Philosophy of Lay Ministry?

Churches will typically involve their members in ministry using one of two approaches: the institutional approach or the individual approach.

An institutional approach to lay ministry begins with the needs of the church institution. Every church needs Sunday school teachers, committee members, and musicians. In the institutional approach, when a role or a position opens up, the response is to search for a person who seems most suitable to fill the job. Success in such churches is when a member says, "OK, I'll take the job." Hopefully the person is qualified, gifted, and motivated for that area of ministry, but there are no guarantees. If it turns out that there was a mismatch between member and task, the predictable result is a task poorly done and the member highly frustrated. "Plugging warm bodies into ministry slots in a congregation," says Pam Heaton, "tends to increase volunteer burnout, dissatisfaction, and departure."[1] With the institutional approach to lay ministry, church members exist to serve the needs of the institution.

The individual approach is far less widely practiced, but far more effective for significant ministry. In this approach, the priority is not so much filling a vacancy as it is identifying a place in which members (and even nonmembers) can find a task that complements their interests and gifts. Rather than beginning with the needs of the institution, the individual approach begins with the strengths of each person. Church members are encouraged to try ministry positions related to their interests and then to see how they fit. If the match is good, the member may choose to spend more time in that ministry and/or to receive additional training. If the task is not comfortable or the person does not feel a sense of calling to it, he or she is encouraged to explore other ministries that might be a better fit. If a natural match cannot be found between existing roles and church members, the possibility of creating a new ministry is explored. In the individual approach to lay ministry, the institution exists for the benefit of the people, rather than the people existing for the benefit of the institution.

Consider this matrix that describes the typical results of these two approaches to lay ministry:

Ministry Measure	Institutional Approach	Individual Approach
Percent of the church community involved in ministry	Less than 20 percent	More than 20 percent
Individual's satisfaction with ministry task	Often frustrated	Usually fulfilled
Personal energy level as a result of the task	Drained	Rejuvenated
Reason for participating	Doing what I must	Doing what I like
Effect on interpersonal church relationships	Friction	Fusion
Number of people declining to serve	Many	Few
Resignations from the task throughout the year	Frequent	Infrequent
Church leaders' motivation for filling the role	Institutional need	Individual growth
Frequency of new ministries created	Seldom	Often

A church's philosophy of lay ministry is not always simple to determine. And rather than an "either-or" way of thinking, it will more likely fall somewhere on a continuum.

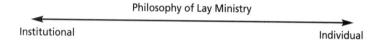

Philosophy of Lay Ministry

Institutional   Individual

Church leaders who wish to create a "greenhouse" for effective lay ministry must consciously keep pushing the church toward the right side of this scale, because the gravitational pull of institutional demands is always to the left. "One of the key challenges facing a pastor is to position the church as a creative place that needs the expression of all sorts of talents and abilities; not just singers, ushers, and Sunday school teachers," says Rick Warren. "One of the reasons enthusiasm is so low in many churches is that creativity is discouraged."[2]

As you can no doubt imagine, starting side doors based on members' interests and passions keeps churches operating and growing at the "individual" end of the ministry continuum.

What Percentage of Your Members Are Involved in Ministry?

The chart below will help you discern whether your church's philosophy of lay ministry facilitates or frustrates the creation of new side doors. To assess your church, begin by filling in the blank at the top left on line 1—your total church constituency. (I know. It reminds me of a tax form, too.) This number represents the size of your overall church family above age thirteen—all members plus regular attendees who are not officially members. Next, calculate the percentages for lines 2–18 and determine in which column your church is located. Determine your percentages based on your total church constituency (line 1) unless otherwise noted.

		Members seen as workers				Members seen as ministers
		Problem	Poor	Average	Good	Ideal
People Involved	1. Total Church Constituency: _____					
	2. Percentage of constituents who have a specific role or task	0–20	21–29	30–49	50–69	70+
	3. Percentage of constituents who have a church-focused role (percentage of number 2)	96+	95–86	85–75	74–61	<60
	4. Percentage of constituents who have an outward-focused role (percentage of number 2)	0–4	5–9	10–14	15–19	20+
	5. Percentage of constituents who attended worship one or more times in the past four months	0–34	35–44	45–59	60–69	70+
	6. Percentage of total number of constituents involved in a small group	0–10	11–29	30–45	46–64	65+
New Attendees	7. Percentage of constituents who began attending in the last twelve months	0–2	3–4	5–6	7–10	11+
	8. Percentage of new constituents (from number 7) who have a role or a task	0–29	30–44	45–59	60–69	70+
	9. Percentage of new constituents (from number 7) who are involved in a small group	0–29	30–49	50–69	70–79	80+
	10. Percentage of constituents who began attending twelve to twenty-four months ago	0–2	3–4	5–6	7–10	11+
	11. Percentage of constituents (from number 10) who have a role or a task	0–29	30–44	45–59	60–69	70+
	12. Percentage of constituents (from number 10) who are involved in a small group	0–29	30–49	50–69	70–79	80+
Ministry	13. Percentage of total roles or tasks available in the church	0–20	21–29	30–49	50–69	70+
	14. Percentage of roles or tasks with a written job description	0–10	11–29	30–50	51–74	75+
	15. Percentage of positions with specific pre-service training	0–10	11–29	30–50	51–69	70+
	16. Percentage of maintenance oriented roles/tasks (from number 13)	90+	89–80	79–70	69–60	<59
	17. Percentage of outreach-oriented roles or tasks (from number 13)	0–8	9–15	16–20	21–34	35+
	18. Percentage of new roles or tasks created in the last twelve months (from number 13)	0–2	3–4	5–6	7–10	11+

Source: *The Growth Report* Vol. 2 No. 6, Institute for American Church Growth (Pasadena, Calif.)

If you find that your church scores fall primarily in the left columns, it is likely that your members are seen as workers and that the focus of your ministry is on the church institution. The farther your scores are to the right, the more likely your members are seen as ministers and that the focus of your ministry is on people. If your scores are predominantly on the right side, it will be much easier to introduce the idea of side doors to your church and find receptivity among the membership.

The Next Step

Chances are good that, having worked through the questions in this chapter, you have concluded that your church would benefit from some new side doors. Such side doors will involve more people in creative and enjoyable ministry and will establish more entry paths for people in your community to become part of your church and the body of Christ.

But there is an important question you will need to answer before you see such new ministries sprouting up in your church. Perhaps it has already crossed your mind: How do you find the people in your church who have the passion, motivation, and desire to begin a new special-interest (side door) ministry? In the next chapter, we're going to get practical about finding that spark of passion. And following that, we'll look at how to fan the spark into a roaring flame.

Getting Started on Your Side Door—Find the Passion

What an insight into God's creativity to consider how different people are from each other, not only physically, but psychologically, intellectually, and emotionally as well. Our cognitive maps are as unique as our fingerprints. We are interested in different things, enthusiastic about different topics, and passionate about different causes. Everyone is interested in something, but the scope of those somethings are as vast as the landscapes of our minds and experiences.

Motivational experts know that the best way to energize people is to tap into something that they already care about. The same holds true for motivating people in the church. An effective system of lay ministry will involve people by matching their interests and passions with activities that complement those interests and passions. A simple but powerful secret to seeing people enthusiastically involved is: channel enthusiasm rather than try to change it.

If you see a generally low level of involvement or satisfaction by the people in your church, the chances are good that you are observing the symptom of one of several problems.

Not Enough *Places* for People to Get Involved

It stands to reason that a church with few ministry positions will have a low percentage of members involved. And if some members take more than one ministry role, even fewer people will be serving. Research has actually found that an ideal role-to-member ratio is approximately sixty to one hundred. That is, in a healthy church there will be approximately sixty places of ministry or service for every one hundred people (members plus regular attendees). When the ratio drops to thirty to one hundred, the church is unhealthy.[1]

Not Enough *Right* Places for People to Get Involved

Imagine that the people in your church represent many different-shaped pegs such as cylinders, cubes, triangular prisms, hexagonal prisms, etc., and that the variety of ministry positions in your church represent various holes shaped as circles, squares, triangles, hexagons, etc. A good lay ministry system will seek to place its various "pegs" into correspondingly shaped "holes," with the assumption that people are best suited to a ministry that fits their shape. Unfortunately, the shape of many churches' ministry holes are limited to triangles and circles. In such churches, lay involvement is low because these churches are trying to force square pegs into round holes since there just aren't enough right places to go around.

Starting new side doors will address both of the above-mentioned problems, as they help you increase the number and variety of ministry positions in your church. But the key is to start with passion.

How to Find the Passion

Everyone in your church cares deeply about something. Most people care about a lot of things. Your members have particular interests, various concerns, and intense passions. Successful side doors are birthed out of what people care about. If you can tap into the passions of your members, you will be like Uncle Jed—he may have missed the rabbit, but he hit something far more valuable: "Up from the ground come a bubblin' crude." If you hit passion in your church, you will strike black gold. (If you were born after 1971, ask your parents about Uncle Jed.)

So how do you do it? First, develop a way to listen for passion in your church on an ongoing basis. "Start where your people are," says the pastor of First Baptist Church in Leesburg, Florida, a church that has transitioned from an institutional to an incarnational approach to lay ministry. "Find the need that most touches their hearts, and they will give themselves to it. Even people who are not directly affected by a problem may feel deeply about it."[2] Think of the guy at the local city park who walks around with his metal detector and headphones listening for a *ping*. Put on your leadership "headphones" and start listening for passion.

My friend, Ricardo Zapata, pastor of Iglesia de los Hermanos Principe de Paz in Santa Ana, California, recently told me about the boys and men in his church who always went to the local park before church to play soccer. Sometimes, he told me, when the game was tied, they would be late for church. "One day it dawned on me," he said. "If I can't beat 'em, I should join 'em." So, he asked several of the men if they would help organize a church soccer league. The idea took off like wildfire.

Here are some ways to identify passion in your people. Perhaps one of them will stir your own creativity.

What You Already Know

If you've been at your church for any length of time, you already know something about the lives of those who attend. Try this exercise: Get ten index cards. Put the name of one person in your church at the top of each card. Below each name jot down anything you are aware of that is important to the person (such as, a family situation, a health concern, a significant life experience, a special interest, etc.). When you are done, look at the cards. On them are clues to possible new side door ministries.

If you decide to enlarge this process beyond ten people (which I suggest you do), store the information on a computer. Create a program or use existing software that lets you store and access specific information about members' passions, interests, concerns, and significant life experiences. This can obviously be helpful in bringing together like-minded people later on.

Life Transitions

One of the constants in life is change. Some change we choose (marriage, relocation, or having children). Other change just happens (aging, losing a job, or having children). Life happens. And not all the things that happen in life feel great. But one of my favorite lifelines is this: God doesn't waste experience. Many side door ministries grow out of tough experiences that people are simply thrust into: having a stroke, being in a car accident, raising a disabled child, or dealing with chronic pain.

One excellent tool for identifying life transitions is the Social Readjustment Rating Scale.[3] Commonly known as a stress scale, this assessment instrument was first developed to predict the risk of heart attacks. It identifies stress-producing events and assigns a number between one and one hundred to indicate the relative stress of each event.

Social Readjustment Rating Scale	
Life Event	**Rank**
1. Death of a spouse	100
2. Divorce	73
3. Marital separation	65
4. Jail term	63
5. Death of a close family member	63
6. Personal injury or illness	53
7. Marriage	50
8. Fired from work	47
9. Marital reconciliation	45
10. Retirement	45
11. Change in health of family member	44
12. Pregnancy	40
13. Sex difficulties	39
14. Gaining a new family member	39
15. Business readjustment	39
16. Change in financial state	38
17. Death of a close friend	37
18. Change to different line of work	36
19. Change in number of arguments with spouse	35
20. A mortgage over $300,000	31
21. Foreclosure of mortgage or loan	30
22. Change in responsibilities at work	29
23. Son or daughter leaving home	29
24. Trouble with in-laws	29
25. Outstanding personal achievement	28
26. Spouse beginning or stopping work	26
27. Beginning or ending school	26
28. Major change in living conditions	25
29. Change in work or sleep habits	24
30. Trouble with boss	23
31. Change in work hours or conditions	20
32. Change in residence	20
33. Change in schools	20
34. Change in recreational pursuits	19
35. Change in church activities	19
36. Change in social activities	18
37. A mortgage or loan less than $300,000	17
38. Change in sleeping habits	15
39. Change in number of family get-togethers	15
40. Change in eating habits	15

As you look at this scale, do you see any events that people in your church have lived through in the last five years? If so, think about the possibility of a side door ministry in your church developed by people who have been there and done that.

I shared this scale at a seminar a few years ago in Ventura, California. At the break, a man in his mid-forties came up to me and said, "You know, there's something missing on this scale that should be rated even higher than losing a spouse."

At first I thought he might be joking, but his face did not show it. "What's that?" I asked.

"The death of a child," he responded, as tears welled in his eyes. He had lost his teenage son to suicide six months earlier. He went on to tell me that he was in the process of working with his pastor to develop a ministry in their church for other families in the community who had lost a child. "Parents are supposed to go before their kids, not after," he said. "It's tough going through something like that. But when you can talk with someone who knows how you feel, it makes a big difference. So that's what I'm going to do through our church—help connect people who need someone to talk to." Now that was a passion-based ministry if I have heard of one!

When people in your church hit life's bumps, they need support. That's one of the wonderful things about being part of Christ's body. Yet a big part of the healing, of coping with those bumps, can be found in helping others over those same bumps—whether they are inside or outside the church. Actually, this process has been going on for years: "God . . . comes alongside us when we go through hard times," wrote the apostle Paul. "And before you know it, he brings us alongside someone else who is going through hard times so that we can be there for that person just as God was there for us" (2 Cor. 1:4 MSG). God doesn't waste experience.

Conversations

It's surprising how many clues about passion we can pick up in simple conversations when we're listening for it. Casual comments, hallway chats, or a conversation after church can provide clues of underlying passion in people. In my experience, enthusiasm is better discovered in casual conversations than by formal delegation. "How many years will it take your committee to decide which affinity group to target?" wonders a responder to a pastoral blog.[4]

I remember being driven to the Louisville airport by a female staff member of a church where I had just finished consulting. I tried a few topics for casual conversation, but nothing seemed to catch. Her responses were short, and she made no effort to nurture the exchange. Then I mentioned something about my teenage son who has ADHD, and the challenge we faced as parents just getting him through an evening's homework. She lit up. Her thirteen-year-old daughter had a similar learning disability. She was frustrated with the school district and was thinking about pulling her child out to do home schooling. But she was divorced and could not afford to be without an income.

Wow! Had I touched a nerve. She couldn't stop talking about all the choices she was facing and how she wished she could talk with someone who either home schooled or who knew of options she might have in the school district. I wondered how many other moms in her church and the community might be in similar situations, and thinking that a topic of so much passion might be a great new ministry. Everyone is passionate about something. It's just a matter of finding the hot button.

Not every passion needs to grow into a new ministry. But every new ministry needs to grow out of passion. When you and other church leaders are thinking of potential new ministries, conversing with people can be like prospecting for gold—listening to, engaging with, and exchanging opinions that could lead to a mother lode of passion.

New Members Orientation

Most pastors believe it is desirable to see new members involved in ministry early in their membership. I agree. The new-members class is a great venue for helping people match their passions with the right ministry. The class also provides a great place to consider starting a new ministry if a good match can't be found for an individual. Of course you'll want to consider how well you know the person and are aware of his or her spiritual maturity and previous experience. But don't try to force your new-member "pegs" into your ministry "holes" if they don't fit. (In the next chapter, we will touch on a team approach to starting new ministries.)

You Are Special! Booklet

Available at my Heartbeat Minstries website (heartbeat ministries.net/downloads) is a set of masters for a 5" x 8" booklet entitled *You Are Special!* This brief resource may be reproduced and used to raise members' awareness that your church is in the "ministry midwife" business—namely, birthing new ministries. The booklet tells the stories of common people who discovered ways to turn their interests into ministries. As they read it, your people will be encouraged to think about their own interests, concerns, and passions and consider whether God might have been preparing them to help start a creative new ministry.

Pastoral Counseling

A pastor friend of mine in Temple City, California, recently told me about a developing side door ministry in his church that was birthed out of a counseling session. A young couple had made an appointment to talk with the pastor about their fourteen-year-old son who had been caught shoplifting for the first time. The parents, of course, were distraught. The pastor knew of another couple in the church with a teenage son who had also had several run-ins with local law enforcement. The pastor asked the young husband and wife if he could introduce them to the other couple.

The two couples, of course, had much in common and became close friends. With the pastor's encouragement, they began exploring whether a support group or some kind of ministry might help other families who were in similar situations.

Interestingly, about three months after the couples had begun talking about such a ministry—and long before any kind of program had been developed—the church began receiving phone calls from people in the community asking about their program for parents with troubled teens. Somehow, just through the couples' casual conversations with friends and neighbors, the idea had spread that this church had a support group for families with problem teens. And the church was getting calls before a program had even been developed. I was reminded of the popular phrase, "The secret to success is to find a need and fill it."

Of course, not every pastoral counseling session will generate a new ministry. But when pastors and lay counselors develop side door sensitivity, it can be another source for turning problems into possibilities. Remember, God doesn't waste experience.

"I Wish . . ." Cards

I got this idea from Lyle Schaller years ago at a workshop. Print some index cards, similar to the one below, and place them in various locations around the church (pew racks, information center, etc.).

Mention these cards periodically in the worship service announcements and in the church newsletter. Review them and then respond to people's suggestions.

"I Wish . . ."

When I think about our church and ways we could make a difference for people in this community, I wish we could have a ministry for . . .

If you would be interested in helping to make your wish come true, write your name and contact information below. (Chances are greatly improved that something will happen if you're willing to be a part.) Then put this card in the offering plate or give it to an usher. We look forward to hearing from you! Thanks.

Name (optional): _____

Phone (optional): _____

E-mail (optional): _____

Congregational Survey

Information about interests, concerns, and passions in your church can also be gathered through a congregational survey. Appendix C provides a sample survey that you are welcome to use or adapt. Categorize people's responses into similar areas of common interest. Through this tool, you'll find many creative ideas for possible side door ministries. For example, you may learn that six people in your church have grandchildren living in their homes. While none of these grandparents may approach you with the idea of a ministry to people in such a situation (nor had they even thought about it), it would be interesting to convene a brief exploratory meeting after church one Sunday for anyone with grandchildren living at home and see what it might produce. Notice that the life events on this survey are the same events that are on the stress scale we looked at earlier. Such common events could be catalysts for building a new side door ministry in your church.

Sermons

A series of sermons can address the fact that every person is unique and has special God-given interests and experiences. Sermons can increase people's sensitivity to the idea that God could be nudging them toward a new ministry.

Jason, a high-school kid in Aumsville, Oregon, showed up at Mountain View Wesleyan Church, asking if he could do community service hours there. He needed only a day or two to meet his requirement. The pastor enlisted Shelby, an older adult church member and resident handyman, to work with Jason doing small projects around the church. The outcome was that Jason worked longer than he needed to, came to church the next Sunday and sat with Shelby, then came back the following week with his younger brother. In the culture of creativity that the pastors had nurtured through their sermons and other means in the church, this experience sparked Shelby's latent desire to help young people, and he is now thinking about starting a mentoring ministry for teenagers.

Finding Passion through Your Website

People can be stimulated to think about starting a new ministry because of your website. Here are some examples of churches that encourage creative thinking online:

- "Ministries begin at Westwood Community Church through the initiative of Westwood attendees and/or staff. If you have the passion to begin a new ministry at Westwood, the process is outlined below . . ." (www.teamwestwood.org).
- "Do you feel like God has placed a desire in you to start a new ministry at Southwest Community Church? We would love to help you build a ministry action plan for your new ministry by completing the following steps . . ." (www.southwestcc.org).
- "Saddleback has many ministries that have been started by lay ministers just like you. So, if you have a possible new ministry idea, please share it with us online so we can see if it qualifies as a new ministry" (www.saddleback.com).
- "Do you feel the desire to start a new ministry at Miracle Temple Seventh-Day Adventist Church? We would love to help you" (www.miracletemple.net).

Make It a Team Effort

The task of listening for passion in your people should be part of the job description of every Bible class teacher, small-group leader, music director, youth leader, and committee chairperson in your church. At your leadership training events, teach your leaders to be passion finders. It's really not hard. Just have them learn to listen for what deeply affects people; to pay attention to what they care about and make note of the things that are big in their lives, either by choice or default.

The McLean Bible Church (Washington, D.C.) stumbled onto a great side door opportunity by being sensitive to people's passions. The ministry began in 1996 when an ad was placed in the church newsletter regarding the formation of a respite ministry for parents of children with disabilities. That lit a spark in the hearts of several people, and the result was a special-needs ministry that now touches more than seven hundred families, both in the church and in the community, who have children with disabilities. They call their ministry Access, and it is one of the premier disabilities ministries in the country. It all started with a few people who were passionate about a human need.

Starting New Ministries in Your Church

While the process of starting a new ministry around one's passion may seem intuitive, if you ask a church member to consider such an undertaking, the response might be something like Moses' response to God: "But why me? What makes you think that I could ever go to Pharaoh and lead the children of Israel out of Egypt?" (Ex. 3:11 MSG). So, you will do your people a great service by providing them with coaching and mentoring.

In the next chapter, we will look at specific steps for building a successful side door. In addition, a free and much more comprehensive resource has been developed. The Side Door Planning Guide is designed specifically for laypersons with step-by-step directions. This guide may be downloaded at www.wphresources.com/sidedoor and duplicated for use in your church.

5

How to Build a Side Door

In this chapter are nine steps that will guide anyone in a church from a ministry dream to an exciting reality. These steps are based on my research of churches that have learned how to build side doors through trial and error, and are now consistently successful. In addition, over one hundred churches have participated in a two-year pilot project of creating new side door ministries. I have tracked the results and identified the best practices. Because side doors provide such tremendous opportunities for effective ministry and outreach, it makes sense to do it right the first time. Here's how . . .

Step 1: Build a Dream Team

In the previous chapter, we discussed the importance of finding people's passions. That is, discovering who in your church cares deeply about something and might be interested in pursuing that passion through starting a new ministry. The passion of at least one person is essential for the birth of a successful special interest ministry. But the passion of one person is not enough. In the early stages of exploring a new ministry, I strongly encourage the formation of two groups.

Prayer Support Team

The prayers of believers have great power and yield wonderful results (see James 5:16). Those who are involved in starting a new ministry will find that their efforts are more productive, their minds sharper, and their hearts softer when fellow Christians are petitioning God to bless their endeavors. I recommend that the commitment of at least five individuals be secured who agree to pray regularly for any new ministry initiative. These individuals should pray that the people starting the new ministry will have vision to see the potential, discernment to make wise choices, compassion for those who will be touched, and resolve when enthusiasm may falter.

Ministry Planning Team

Starting a new ministry is not a one-runner marathon; it is a multi-runner relay. One visionary can't do it alone, shouldn't try to do it alone, and shouldn't be allowed to do it alone. A group of three to five people should work together in starting every new ministry. One church I know of uses the term *ministry planning team* to describe their planning groups. With the church's permission, I have adopted this term and will use it throughout the remainder of the book. Of course, you can call your planning groups whatever you'd like. The important thing is what they do, not what they are called.

As a new ministry is given birth, this group of like-minded people encourage each other, generate creative ideas, and, hopefully, get things done more effectively and efficiently. Those invited to be on the ministry planning team should obviously share a passion for the idea behind the ministry. But, in addition to present church members, I have found that it is a good idea to enlist several team members (perhaps friends or relatives) who are not part of the church. This can provide a helpful balance and provide the group with a perspective on how to best connect with unchurched people.

A planning team is so important to ultimately realizing a successful new ministry that if at least three people cannot be found who will work together in starting the new ministry, I recommend that further plans be suspended until such a team can be assembled.

Step 2: Research Other Ministries

Chances are good that creative churches around the country have ministries similar to the one your ministry planning team is envisioning. Thus, one of the team's most productive early activities will be to learn from these churches.

A two-hour Internet research session will yield a plethora of information and stimulate ideas for the new ministry. Google one or more words that describe the topic. Include *church* as a key word. Another helpful modifier is *ministry*. Experiment with different word combinations.

Internet research should also include Amazon with the same search criteria. Make a note of any books, videos, or other possibly helpful resources you find on the subject. If an author has written on the topic, buy the book. If the author is on the staff of a church, he or she would probably be happy to answer questions that will help streamline your church's start-up.

Model Church Ministries

During the research, several churches will likely surface as particularly stellar examples of the kind of ministry your planning team is envisioning. To avoid reinventing the wheel, the group should seek out several model church ministries and schedule a telephone interview with a knowledgeable person from the church. A Model Church Summary form is provided in appendix D that will help guide the team in this interview and summary process.

Organize Your Insights

Ministry planning teams should keep a notebook for organizing their research and interviews. Divider tabs can be labeled in the following order:

- Case Study Church 1: [fill in church name]
- Case Study Church 2: [fill in church name]
- Case Study Church 3: [fill in church name]
- Related Organizations
- Websites
- Articles
- Books
- People and Contacts

More information on how to prepare for, conduct, and summarize the research is included in the Side Door Planning Guide.

Step 3: Describe the Target Audience

Successfully starting a new ministry requires a clear understanding of the people who will be affected by that new ministry.

Mark Howell, founder of smallgroupresources.net, says that clearly defining your target audience is "very big." Launching a new ministry "without understanding who the ministry is designed to serve almost always leads to a miss."[1]

Get Specific

Here is a key principle: The more specifically you describe your target audience, the more successful your ministry will be. For example, compare these two target group descriptions and see which one would be more likely to catch a person's interest:

- Women
- Women between twenty-five and forty, divorced, with children at home, who are experiencing financial difficulties

The first group includes more than half the population in your church and your community. One might think that with so many potential participants—all women in the area—it would be easy to get a crowd. In reality, just the opposite is true. Such a broad definition makes it nearly impossible to provide a need-meeting ministry to everyone who happens to be a woman.

The second target group definition is quite specific and identifies five different qualities (gender, age, marital status, family status, special need). It is easy to imagine what kind of need-meeting activities a new ministry that was focused on this target group might provide. If you were a person who was in the second target group, you would certainly be interested in learning more about a group or activity that could help make your quality of life better. And you would likely bond very quickly with other women in such a group who shared your life situation.

More Than Meets the Eye

As the ministry planning team considers their target audience and who will be touched by the new ministry, they may discover that it will affect more people than they originally realized. For example, today the Messiah Lutheran Church (Yorba Linda, California) has a wonderful ministry called Homework House where adult tutors work with students who are not progressing well in school. The planning team's initial target audience was kids struggling academically. But they soon realized that there were two other groups who would also be touched by the new ministry: (1) the parents and families of children being tutored, and (2) adult tutors who were not church members but were working hand in hand with Messiah members.

The chart below can help clarify the target group(s) for a new ministry. Not all the areas in the far left column may be important in the definition, but it is worthwhile to consider each of them.

	Your Target Audience	Others Affected
Age Range		
Marital Status		
Family Status		
Interests/Hobbies		
Concerns/Problems		
Ethnic/Cultural Identity		
Financial Status		
Other Characteristics		

Step 4: Define the Purpose

A clear purpose statement for the new ministry is essential. A purpose statement should answer three simple questions: What are we doing? Why are we doing it? How are we doing it?

Todd Pridemore, an expert in starting side door ministries in his church, says, "Make sure everyone understands the primary purpose of this new ministry: *reaching unchurched people*. It is extremely easy for this new activity to evolve into nothing more than a fellowship group or social club for church members."[2] Of course, the new ministry should not be *exclusively* outward-focused; your own church members should participate in the group, as well. But if the new ministry is made up entirely of Christians and church members, it will become a diversion of your church's resources from its primary mission: "Go and make disciples" (Matt. 28:19).

Sample Purpose Statements

Here are some purpose statements of side door ministries. Notice how each statement clearly defines the church's target audience and how each one is designed to include people both inside and outside the church:

- HopeKeepers is a group for those dealing with a recent medical diagnosis, chronic illness, and/or pain. Together, we share prayer requests and questions. Meetings are held twice a month and are open to all friends and family (Lake Avenue Church, Pasadena, California).
- The goal of the Crisis Care Ministry is to provide assistance and resources to individuals in crisis—within and outside of PEPC—and to help them gain independence, self-sufficiency, and a closer spiritual relationship with Christ. Crisis is defined as an acute situation requiring immediate assistance (Parker Evangelical Presbyterian Church, Parker, Colorado).
- Nathaniel's Hope Buddy Break is a ministry dedicated to sharing hope with kids who have special needs (VIP kids) and their families (Calvary Assembly of God, Winter Park, Florida).
- C.R.U.I.S.E. Motorcycle Ministry leads fellow bikers and motorcycle enthusiasts toward a closer relationship with Jesus Christ and each other. Our mission is to ride safely as a group in Christian fellowship and as an outreach team for our Lord (Hickory Grove Baptist Church, Charlotte, North Carolina).
- Break Free was established to be a ministry of hope and healing from the isolation, anxiety, fear, and shame that accompany chemical dependency. The ministry provides an opportunity for people to participate in a Christ-centered, twelve-step process that is biblically based, nondenominational, clinically tested, and proven to provide important tools that an addicted person needs to make a complete recovery from chemical addiction (Grove City Church of the Nazarene, Grove City, Ohio).

Step 5: Determine the Strategy

Now the fun begins. This step is all about preparing and planning the new ministry. The Ministry Planning Chart (appendix E) will help the planning team organize their activities most strategically at this point. The discussion below refers to the individual components of this chart. You will want to flip back and note the chart as you read the following. (When the chart is actually used by a planning group, it should be transposed onto several flip charts, leaving room to write.)

Target Audience

In step 3, the ministry planning team identified their target audience. This description should simply be transferred to the planning chart. The chart is divided into two halves: the left side applies to the target audience—those for whom the new ministry is intended. The right side applies to any others who will be affected—those indirectly influenced by the new ministry.

Once the target audience(s) has been recorded, planning the new ministry for these people will focus on three levels: felt needs, deeper needs, and eternal needs.

Stage 1: Felt Needs

The first connection between the church and the target audience should be around their felt needs. Getting this right is very important. It is not the planning team's opinion of the felt needs, it is the target audience's own assessment. Thus, face-to-face interviews with people in the target group will greatly assist the planning team in seeing the world through the eyes of those in the target group. (The Side Door Planning Guide includes extensive guidelines for how to get accurate information on a target audience.)

Earlier I mentioned Homework House, a ministry of Messiah Lutheran Church that focuses on tutoring academically needy children. Their planning team's research indicated that the felt needs of these kids (their target group) were: (1) a desire to be successful in school, (2) a fear of being called stupid by classmates, and (3) having a sense of insecurity and a low self-image. The research found that the felt needs of the parents (others affected, as identified on the Ministry Planning Chart) included: (1) a concern for their children's academic performance, (2) a lack of time to help their children with homework, and (3) a desire to see their children develop strong self-esteem. If your new ministry provides a genuine response to actual felt needs, people in the target group will be very interested in what you have to offer. However, if a felt need is not correctly identified, the first gathering of the new ministry will feel very lonely.

Next, set one or more specific goals that will respond to those identified felt needs. In the case of Homework House, the church's specific goal was to establish an after-school tutoring program from 3:00 p.m. to 5:00 p.m., Monday through Thursday. Their secondary goal was to develop a presentation that would introduce parents to the tutoring program so they would feel comfortable allowing their children to attend. The presentation would address the three felt needs they had identified among parents.

The final activity in stage 1 is to identify the steps by which these goals will be reached. This is simply a matter of answering the question, How do we get from here to there? Appendix F provides a Goal Planning Worksheet that one church developed. I like it because it helps identify the various tasks, people, costs, and deadlines involved in accomplishing the goal.

Stage 2: Deeper Needs

While felt needs are important to people for a while, once met, they lose their significance. If felt needs are the only reason people come to your church's new ministry, when the felt need goes away, so will the people. However, a new ministry has the potential to go far beyond meeting felt needs. A new ministry can touch the essence of the human spirit. Stage 2 focuses on meeting people's deeper needs by nurturing deeper relationships among participants.

Let's expand on the list of deeper human needs introduced in chapter 2. Think about how the people in your new ministry can have these deeper needs met:

- People feel disconnected and isolated; they are looking for a place to belong and to feel as if they are part of a family or community.
- People feel the pressure of a busy and stressful world; they are looking for a sense of balance and for ways to manage priorities.
- People sense the shallowness of superficial encounters with others; they are looking for authentic relationships.
- People feel empty and drained from striving to meet their desires through work, material possessions, or entertainment; they are looking for spiritual answers to their unfulfilled hunger.
- People feel overwhelmed by the pace of change in every aspect of their world; they are looking for help through transitions.

In stage 2, the simple goal is to nurture relationships among those who have become involved in the new ministry. As relationships grow, these deeper needs can be met. As a result of these deepening relationships, participants will no longer attend only because their surface needs are being met. They will attend because the gathering of former strangers that they have become part of will have become a community of caring people, and they will experience a sense of belonging that is very rare in our world today. On the Ministry Planning Chart (appendix E), I have suggested the goal for stage 2: To build increasingly meaningful and caring relationships among those touched by this ministry (both church members and nonmembers). The place on the chart to identify how this goal will be achieved is left blank to be completed by the ministry planning team.

Stage 3: Eternal Needs

Stage 3, planning for people's eternal needs, simply takes the plans in stage 2 (meeting deeper needs) to a spiritual level. Put simply, the progression from stage 1 to stage 2 to stage 3 is a progression from acquaintances to friendships to love. It is the process of helping people experience God's love through the love of God's people.

In stage 3 of the Ministry Planning Chart, I have suggested the following goal: To help those affected by our ministry to grow in their understanding and experience of God's love. The planning question here is how to help people experience the genuine presence and love of God. Christianity is all about God's love for us and our love for God expressed through our love for others (see Matt. 22:37–40). There is no command given in the Bible more often than the command to love. Stage 3 of the ministry planning process intentionally implements the words of the apostle John: "Let's not just talk about love; let's practice real love" (1 John 3:18 MSG).

Step 6: Publicize Your Ministry

Wouldn't it be nice to have people show up at the first gathering of your new ministry? Yet every church has had meetings with a disappointing turnout despite an excellent program. A poorly attended meeting, especially when it's the first gathering of a new venture, is no fun. In fact, it can be downright discouraging.

In publicizing the first public event of the new ministry, keep in mind that there are two groups in the target audience: those who are presently in the church and those who are not. It is more challenging, as you can imagine, to communicate with and involve those who are not part of the church. But remember, the goal is that between 25 percent and 75 percent of the participants are nonmembers. And, of course, this aspect of the group will be most important to its long-term success.

Below are five marketing strategies that will help publicize your new ministry, especially the first meeting.

Strategy 1: Decide Why the Benefit Is Worth the Price

People who consider attending an event will subconsciously ask the question, "What is the benefit, and what is the cost?" "What is the promise, and what is the price?" As you publicize the event, highlight the benefits of attending. Or, as someone has so aptly said, "Sell the sizzle." Effective promotion will convince prospective attendees that the risk of attending the event is worth the benefit they will receive.

For most people, one of the biggest "costs" of attending an event is time. Their schedules are full, and they are not looking for one more thing to do. The question people will have that you will need to answer in your publicity is, "Why should I rearrange my schedule to attend your meeting?"

Strategy 2: Produce a Nice Color Brochure

The more people you want to attend your gathering, the nicer your brochure should be. The least desirable approach is to use clip art from a desktop publishing program and design a brochure yourself. A better approach is to buy preprinted template brochures at a local stationery store, add your own copy to them, and print them on a laser printer. The best approach is to secure the services of a professional designer who can help you develop an attractive brochure to "sell the sizzle" as you invite people to your activity.

Strategy 3: Personal Invitations Work Better Than Mass Invitations

If you send advertisements by mail, a good bulk mailing will generate approximately a 0.5 percent return. That is, for every two hundred fliers you send out, one person will show up. By contrast, personal invitations will generate a 25 percent to 30 percent return; for every two hundred personal invitations extended (from someone whom the recipient knows), fifty to sixty people will come. Personal invitations are effective, inexpensive, and involve more people in the promotional effort. You certainly do need a nice flier or brochure for your new ministry, but mass mailing the brochure should never take the place of a personal invitation. In fact, the best use of brochures is to have people give them personally to friends and relatives.

Strategy 4: Provide for Multiple Exposures

The target audience should hear about the event more than once. The more often people hear about it, the more likely it is that they will come. Research shows that a group of people can see or hear the same message up to seven times, and with each exposure more will decide to come. The planning team should ask how they are going to get the message out multiple times.

Strategy 5: Use Multiple Media

The number of times people hear a message is important (as we just saw in strategy 4). But so is the number of *ways* people hear a message. The more senses that are involved in receiving a message, the more likely it is that the message will be remembered. Some people are auditory learners, others are visual or tactile. Be imaginative in using different kinds of communication media when extending an invitation. Don't send the same flier three or four times; be creative.

The Publicity Planning Worksheet (appendix G) will help identify and schedule the tasks, people, and time required to publicize the event. If it appears that the time required to adequately publicize the event is more than the time before the first gathering, I suggest the meeting be postponed. You don't have a second chance at a successful first meeting. And the success of that meeting will be crucial in establishing momentum for the future.

Step 7: Prepare for the First Meeting

The first gathering of your new ministry will set the tone for future meetings and greatly influence whether people come back. There is only one opportunity for a good first impression. In planning for the first meeting, consider the following details.

Hosts

Plan to have at least one host for every five to eight people expected. Hosts should greet those who arrive and engage them in conversation. If a guest arrives alone and doesn't seem to know anyone, a good host will spend time with the person and introduce him or her to others.

Name Tags

Use name tags at every meeting; peel-off labels work the best. Have a supply of felt-tip pens. Hosts should wear a name tag and give name tags out as people arrive.

Room Preparation

Table and chair setup should facilitate social interaction (a horseshoe or circle works best or round tables). Chairs should not be so close that they intrude into people's personal space. Consider decorating tables or walls in a theme that underscores the purpose of the meeting.

Refreshments

Punch, coffee, cookies, etc. should be available when people arrive.

Icebreaker

There will be people at your meeting who won't know each other (hopefully many of them). Relationships can be started with something as simple as a creative (but not corny) icebreaker. There are many ideas on the Internet. Choose an activity that does not take too long but that gets people talking and laughing. (It's a good idea to have an icebreaker activity to begin each subsequent meeting, as well.)

Handouts

Prepare a handout summarizing the purpose of the group, what you hope to accomplish, the general organization of the group, when and where you will meet, number of meetings, length of each meeting, etc.

Getting Acquainted

The first time the group meets, have people introduce themselves to each other early in the meeting. Think about what things people could tell the group about themselves; perhaps some interesting or unusual facts about their lives. But don't make the topics too personal.

Relationship Building

The people who come to the initial meeting will be hoping that the promise is worth the price. Be prepared to deliver on the promise of meeting felt needs. At the same time, help people feel comfortable with each other and with the possibility of making new friends. The goal is to create a "greenhouse" environment in the first meeting where relationships can flourish and grow in the future.

Group Ownership

While the ministry leaders are responsible to direct the group, participants should also have input into the agenda and activities. Leaders should be open to—and even seek out—suggestions for group topics and activities. The mission and purpose of the group can be accomplished in many different ways. Share ownership.

Step 8: Plan for Long-Term Benefits

Nurturing social community is key to a successful new ministry. Participants already share similarities with others because of their common interest, so encouraging relational bonding should not be difficult.

Here is a brief description of what I call the two-step—a way of achieving our earlier-mentioned goals of meeting people's deeper, as well as eternal, needs.

With the two-step we start short, then go long. This refers to the length of time the group will meet. Here's how it works.

Start Short

The ideal number of times a new group should gather is between six and ten. Sociologically, six is the minimum number of contacts necessary for a collection of people to become a group of people. On the other end, ten meetings is about the most that people will commit to without knowing anything about the group. So in your first gathering, remind participants how many times your group will be meeting. (This information should have also been in your publicity.) Explain that when the group approaches its final few meetings, participants can discuss whether they want to continue meeting or not.

In each of the scheduled meetings, spend time building relationships and developing a sense of camaraderie among the group members. In the first six to ten meetings, don't expect deep friendships to develop. But it is likely that participants will get to know each other, start remembering names (be sure to use name tags at each meeting), and enjoy being together. Don't force community, but encourage and facilitate it.

Getting-to-Know-You Questions

Here are a few examples of simple questions to help participants get to know each other:

- Where would you like to go if money or time were no object?
- What is a pleasant memory from your childhood?
- When have you been afraid, and why?
- What is one thing that really irritates you? One thing that makes you happy?
- Have you ever had a great idea for a product or service that could make you millions?
- What do you like and dislike about your job?

With each subsequent meeting, assuming relationships continue to be nurtured, the sense of community among participants will grow. Eventually, in the second or third month, the value of the relationships among group members will come to be perceived as being as valuable as the content of your meetings. At that point an amazing thing will have occurred—a group will have been born.

Go Long

Now for the second part of the two-step. In the group's next-to-last scheduled gathering, ask participants to think about what they would like to do in terms of the future. Indicate that the question will be discussed at the following and final meeting, and a decision about whether to continue meeting will be up to them.

At the final meeting ask participants for feedback on the highs and lows of the group. Discuss whether the group members want to continue meeting or to stop. Explain that if the group were to continue meeting, everyone need not participate: new people could be invited and others could freely leave. The group may want to review its purpose and/or its activities. With the destiny of the group in members' hands, an important sense of ownership and identity will emerge that will be important for the long term.

If the group decides to disband, thank participants for their participation and close the meeting in prayer. If the group decides to continue meeting (which is likely), here are some ideas for continuing to nurture the growing sense of relational community.

Go to Special Events Together. In addition to the regular gatherings, if there are activities that sound fun to the group, encourage the participants to attend together. Such events not only provide fun activities, but give group members more common experiences to strengthen relationships. See a movie, go hear a popular speaker, attend a church- or community-sponsored event, work on a service project, or eat out together.

Have a Party. There's always a good reason for a party. Maybe it's a birthday, a new baby, a wedding engagement, a military vet returning, a job promotion, or any combination of these. People who are so honored feel affirmed, and all those celebrating feel closer to each other.

Help Someone in Need. Working together to benefit someone in need is a great way to build long-term relationships. When a need becomes known, whether a family member, friend, or someone in the community, ask the ministry participants if they would be interested in helping respond to it. A common and powerful bond develops when people work together to clean up the yard of an older widow or go shopping for school supplies with kids from a needy family or bring food to a mom and baby just home from the hospital. One of the best ways to learn about God's love is to be a channel of that love to others.

Step 9: Evaluate and Enlarge the Ministry

At some point, the new ministry should be evaluated. Questions that leaders should ask and honestly answer include:

- Has the new group or ministry worked the way organizers had hoped?
- What has been learned in the process of beginning the new ministry?
- Now that the ministry has a history, which of the following options seems best?
  - Enlarge the ministry's influence to touch more people
  - Focus on improving the existing ministry
  - Call it quits
  - Other

Planning an Entry Event

An entry event is a high visibility activity or event, sponsored by your church and designed to be of interest to churched and unchurched people in the ministry's target audience. The purpose of an entry event is to introduce your church's ministry to prospective new participants in the community. The list below illustrates some ideas for entry events based on the target audience.

Target Audience	Entry Event
Parents of adolescents	Father-daughter Valentine's banquet
Sports enthusiasts	Super Bowl Sunday
Newlyweds	One-day conference with workshops, display booths, panel discussion, entertainment, etc.
Families in which both parents work	Saturday-night family taffy pull
Single parents	Trip to a local sports game
Golfers	Golf tournament
People needing financial help	Tax-planning workshop
Recent divorcees	One-day seminar on financial management
New neighbors	"Welcome to the Neighborhood" day

How to Plan a Successful Entry Event

1. Enlist a Planning Team. The best people to plan an entry event are the ones who share a passion for which the new ministry was formed. This will most likely include those who are presently involved in your ministry but should also include some nonmembers.

2. Select an Event That Addresses a Felt Need. The prospective attendees will be asking the same cost-benefit question discussed earlier. So in deciding what kind of event to put on, be sure it offers enough benefit for the cost.

3. Publicize the Event. When people see publicity for the entry event, it will be the first time most of them will have heard about your ministry. So when you go public, do it with quality. Your publicity will go a long way toward positioning the new ministry in the minds of the those who see it.

4. Select the Best Location. Consider holding the high-visibility event somewhere other than at your church. Your goal is not to get people onto your church campus, but rather to establish a connection for building relationships. Unless you have an exceptional facility, possible locations could be a room in the public library, a local school, a community center, a town hall, a city park, etc.

5. Obtain Participants' Contact Information. People who attend the entry event will likely be open to future related activities. To obtain their contact information so that you can send them invitations for future events, ask everyone who attends to fill out a registration card. Some churches offer door prizes donated by church members or businesses in the community, with winners being drawn from the submitted registration cards.

6. Introduce Your Ministry. Provide a "next step" for those who are interested in learning more about the new ministry. Invite them to the next activity. Distribute an informative brochure with time, date, and directions. Give people an opportunity to be added to an e-mail list for announcements of future events. Make it easy for people to take the next step toward getting more involved.

The Single Message

A quality entry event will attract people. But regardless of the kind of event, one message should be communicated—the message of hope. Hope helps people face the future with optimism. While hope does not deny there are problems, hope helps people handle those problems. For the unchurched man or woman, the idea that there may be a way to make sense out of a seemingly senseless life is a tantalizing prospect. An entry event that carries a message of hope conveys to people that life can be better and that change can happen—that a meaningful, significant, purposeful existence may really be possible.

Hope can be communicated through a testimony from a church member, a brief devotional from the pastor, a prayer, a panel discussion, or printed literature. Don't give a hard-sell evangelistic pitch, but try to give participants a little taste of the water, which will cause them to never thirst again (see John 4:14).

Follow-Up the Contacts

If you obtained peoples' names and addresses, follow-up with them. Mail a brochure and a "thanks for attending" note. Invite people to another activity of interest. Expand the variety of groups and activities within your new ministry. And begin planning another entry event.

A Ministry Coach
Your Side Door Contractor

Churches that create a "greenhouse" in which members are released to grow their passion into a creative ministry do not depend on the pastor to tend that greenhouse. Successful side door churches have a go-to person who oversees the process of starting and growing new ministries. Alan Nelson, in his popular book *Me to We*, says, "Every church should have someone besides the pastor who will champion the equipping value and develop ministry teams to implement the process."[1] He's right. I call this person a ministry coach.

What Is a Ministry Coach?

A ministry coach is your church's "contractor" for overseeing the construction of successful side doors. He or she understands the philosophy and importance of side doors as part of the church's ministry and provides guidance and accountability to those involved in pursuing their passion.

The coach does not build the side door ministries; that's the work of the ministry planning team. Rather, the coach is the person who has a bird's-eye view of the overall side door strategy of the church.

The ministry coach may be full time (for a larger church) or part time, paid or volunteer. This role may be added to the portfolio of someone already serving the church in some capacity. The position may even be filled by several people who work together as ministry coaches.

Qualifications

A good ministry coach needs to be someone in whom the pastor has confidence, respect, and trust. If the pastor is going to delegate authority to the coach, then the pastor must have assurance that the oversight of creating new church ministries is in good hands.

In addition to being trustworthy, the ministry coach must be committed to the church's philosophy of lay ministry and enthusiastic about community outreach. A good ministry coach will have the spiritual gift of administration, be able to encourage people, and be able to hold people accountable to goals, budgets, and deadlines.

What Does the Ministry Coach Do?

The rest of this chapter is a sort of job description for a ministry coach. The coach's responsibilities can be organized into three areas, which we will examine further:

- Identify passion and potential for new ministries in the church;
- Support the people involved in starting a new ministry; and
- Communicate with the pastor, church leaders, and ministry planning teams so that everyone is informed about the new endeavor.

Let's examine each of these three areas.

Identify Passion and Potential

The ministry coach's first and ongoing task is to let people in the congregation know that it's OK to dream about a new ministry. In fact, it's OK to do more than dream—it's OK to pursue that dream. And people will act on their dreams when they know that the church will help them in that pursuit. "We try to find out what our church members enjoy doing, apart from attending worship and going to Bible study," says Todd Pridemore. "We encourage people to think outside the box. There is almost no activity so secular that it cannot be used to create a side door into our church."[2]

Find the Passion. In chapter 4, we discussed the importance of finding people with passion. The ministry coach is constantly in search of people whose experience may be just the key to starting a new ministry. God doesn't waste experience.

How to Find Passion

Here are some ways the ministry coach can facilitate "passion prospecting" in a church:

- Teach church members about the importance of finding a ministry—or creating one—in the new members' class.
- Place "I Wish" cards on information tables, in visitor packets, in pew backs, on brochure racks and mention them regularly (see page 76).
- Encourage the pastor to preach a series of messages on lay ministry and on each member's unique role in the body of Christ.
- Conduct a congregational survey to identify the interests and passions of people in the church (see appendix C).
- Use the church newsletter and worship services to highlight new ministry initiatives that members are already taking.
- Ask small group leaders and class teachers to listen for interests, needs, or experiences in people's lives that could be the basis of a new ministry.
- Conduct periodic new ministry conversations after church—fifteen-minute brainstorming sessions to consider a specific topic and whether anyone has an interest in helping start a ministry in this area. Such conversations can grow out of an analysis of the congregational survey or can be called by anyone in the church concerning a need and opportunity they have seen.

Conduct Talking-Points Interviews. An early step in birthing a new ministry will be a formal conversation between the ministry coach and the visionary. I call this conversation a talking-points interview. It is an opportunity to explore the idea behind a new ministry, to consider the need, evaluate its possibilities, and think about the people who could be involved. A list of questions to guide this interview is available in appendix H (Talking Points Discussion Guide).

This person, if he or she was to start a new ministry, would represent your church and be part of the church's public image in the community. So, it is important to be sure that you have both the right idea and the right person. The ministry coach should invite an additional person to sit in on this meeting in order to have a second set of ears, as well as be a source for later debriefing. (This additional person is particularly important if the ministry coach and interviewee are different genders.) Prior to your interview, give the potential ministry leader a copy of the Talking-Points Discussion Guide (appendix H) so that he or she can anticipate the questions that will be asked.

The ministry coach should treat this conversation like a job interview. Look at how the person dresses and communicates. Was he on time for the meeting? Is she enthusiastic about her idea? Does he seem to have the people skills to make this happen? Does she have a desire to reach new people for Christ, or just focus on people in the church? And having reviewed the Talking-Points Discussion Guide before the meeting, did the person come prepared with thoughtful answers?

In the interview, the visionary should know that it is the policy of the church to run a background check on anyone who represents the church. Is he or she OK with that? (A good source for background checks is Group Publishing, www.group.com).

Toward the conclusion of the talking-points discussion, make a list of next steps. If the ministry coach is uncertain about giving the interviewee a green light to proceed, the next step could be to schedule a second meeting. Give the interviewee a few assignments, such as talking with others who might be interested in helping with the new ministry. Encourage the person to bring some of those interested people to the next meeting.

While the ministry coach may have some questions about the qualifications or leadership skills of the person, don't underestimate the power of enthusiasm and vision. There are many exceptional ministries in churches today that were started by people with little experience or charismatic leadership. But these people believed so strongly in their vision, and pursued it with such enthusiasm, that they became the spark for a unique new ministry and a significant side door into their church.

In the talking-points interviews, don't feel that every person must be given a go-ahead. While there is nothing better than an enthusiastic person passionately pursuing a new ministry, there can be nothing worse than a misguided person making public missteps in the name of your church. I am reminded of my father's advice to me in my courting days: "Marry in haste, repent at leisure." He was telling me to be sure that I was picking the right person in going into a long commitment. I offer the same advice. You are not required to give anyone the authority to act under the auspices of the church. Not only are you putting the church's reputation on the line, but you will be involving the church's legal liability, as well. Be in contact with your church's attorney anytime there is a question regarding possible liability issues. You need confidence in the people who will be representing your church.

If there is consensus among the church leadership that you have both the right idea and the right person, the interviewee should be given a copy of the Side Door Planning Guide. Go over the guide with the person, and point out the importance of following the process outlined in it. The person should first read the entire study guide and then begin working on the first step: identifying both a ministry planning team and a prayer support team. Once a ministry planning team has been assembled, the person should schedule a meeting with the ministry coach to go over the next steps and to reaffirm the church's support for this upcoming venture.

Support New Ministry Leaders

In addition to continuously prospecting for passion among members, another responsibility of the ministry coach is to encourage and help those who are already pursuing their passion in a new ministry. Just as a newborn needs special attention in its first months of life, so those nursing the new vision need that same kind of attention and support.

The First Crucial Months. The ministry planning team will be navigating uncharted territory as it sets out in pursuit of its dream. It is to everyone's advantage that the ministry coach and ministry planning team stay in close communication in the early stages of the journey.

The ministry coach should be proactive in contacting the team. The coach should help the planning team with research and pass along information on websites, churches with similar ministries, related books, organizations, and other helpful resources. If a person (in- or outside the church) is identified as someone with related experience, the name should be sent to the planning team for follow-up.

It is encouraging for the church to provide scholarships to ministry planning team members who wish to attend a relevant training conference. For example, my wife is currently beginning a ministry in our church for families of children with special needs. Our church paid for her ministry planning team to attend a Joni and Friends Conference in our area. Her team was greatly encouraged both by the conference and our church's support of the new ministry.

The ministry coach should create an electronic file for each new ministry. This should include copies of e-mails, notes of any comments, questions, or concerns following phone conversations, and other related information. This file will be important for reports to the pastor and to church leadership, and be useful if any complications develop down the road. In other words, create a paper trail.

The ministry coach should publicly affirm the planning team and prayer support team for their vision and commitment. Worship services are an excellent context in which to say, "We support you." In so doing, the ministry pioneers will be encouraged, and others in the church will reflect on their own passions and ministry possibilities.

Three Important Priorities. In my research of churches around the country, I have identified three critical areas in which new ministries can get off course. The ministry coach should keep these three issues in front of every ministry planning team. Just as the loss of one leg from a three-legged stool causes it to come crashing down, each of these three issues are critical for a new ministry to become a successful side door into your church. It is easier to address these issues earlier than to fix them later.

First, be outward focused. When church people start new groups, they have a tendency to recruit participants exclusively from within the church. Don't let the ministry planning team make this mistake. Those involved in planning the new ministry should give much attention and effort to connecting with unchurched people from the outset. A new ministry that is comprised only of church members will set an inward-focused precedent that will be very difficult to change.

Of course, there will be some people in the church who have an interest in the new ministry and want to participate in it, and they should be encouraged to do so. But the team's planning for the new ministry should work toward assuring that nonmembers will be at the first and all subsequent gatherings. The ministry coach should keep this outward-focused thinking in front of every ministry planning team and regularly ask team members how they are doing at including nonmembers in their activities. If involving nonmembers is not an early and constant priority, the side door will close and lock.

In addition to unchurched people, three other people groups should be invited to participate in the ministry's initial and subsequent activities: recent church visitors, new church members, and less-active church members.

Newcomers (visitors or new members) are still on the relational fringes of the church's social network and are hoping to make new friends. Involvement in a new ministry can be the perfect solution—it provides the ministry with enthusiastic participants, and it helps newcomers make friends around common interests. Of course, not every new church attendee will be interested in participating in the new ministry. But the ministry coach should give the names and contact information of all recent church visitors, new attendees, and new members to the planning team, which should then be followed up with a personal invitation.

Concerning inactive members, research indicates that dropouts do not generally return to a church they have left. But a new ministry initiative, particularly if it involves a person's strongly held need or interest, can be a good reason for some inactives to try the church again. It may well begin their journey toward reconciliation with lost friends and the Christian community. It never hurts to invite these people.

Second, provide spiritual exposure. A second way that side doors can get stuck is when a new ministry does not develop an effective spiritual dynamic. "The most significant thing to consider is what can be done so that those unchurched people who have entered your side door will have the opportunity to experience and respond to God as they feel led to do so," observes Todd Pridemore.[3] Your new ministry is not simply a class on car repair or a group for craft making. While repairing cars or making crafts could be a great focus for a new ministry, the ministry planning team should understand that these activities are not the ultimate reason for the ministry.

Every gathering of the new ministry should be an opportunity for participants to have some exposure to God and to his people. For example, a Baptist church in Riverside, California, began a children's photography group as a new ministry conceived by a professional photographer in the church. Twice a month on Saturday mornings the parents and kids gather at the church for a lesson in cameras and photography. Each child in the class receives a disposable digital camera. Following the lesson the group leaves on a field trip to practice their new photography skills. But before they leave, the leader gives a short talk about capturing the beauty of God's creation and how God's special fingerprint can be seen and photographed if they look closely for it. Then one of the children from the church prays for God's protection before they depart. A good way to bring spirituality into the picture.

Another example of building a spiritual dynamic into a side door ministry is Pump 'n Praise, a women's aerobics group created by two young moms at Wheaton Bible Church. The group was designed as a fifty-minute aerobic exercise program suited for women of most abilities and choreographed to contemporary Christian music. Following their exercise session, they "share prayer requests and praises as [they] exercised the power of prayer."[4]

The Glendora Church of the Brethren began a new ministry when several church members were given permission to dig up part of the church's side yard and turn it into a garden. Members in the community were invited to join in the digging and planting. Six months later, at their first "eat-in," the pastor led the group in a thanksgiving prayer before the thirty gardeners (two-thirds of whom were not church members) enjoyed the fruits of their labors.

Research supports the need for multiple exposures to the gospel in the process of effective disciple making. A doctoral dissertation at University of Illinois compared people who had made a faith commitment and become active church members with others who had also made a Christian decision but later dropped out. The researcher found that those who remained active in a church had been exposed to the Christian message at least six different times *before* their decision to follow Christ. On average, those who had dropped out had been exposed to the Christian message only twice prior to their decision. The researcher concluded that those who had been exposed to the gospel multiple times had a far better understanding of what their commitment really involved.[5]

If the goal is disciple-making and not just decision-making, provide many different opportunities for non-believers to see and hear what it means to be a Christ follower. If people in the groups decide to follow Christ, the chances go up dramatically that they will be active in your church for years to come.

Third, intentionally nurture relationships. A third priority for every new ministry—and an area in which some groups stumble— is to intentionally create and nurture deep relationships among participants. Relationships are the glue that keep people connected. When meaningful relationships are not nurtured, that glue is weakened and loses its bond.

A research study recorded the number of close friends that active church members had made in the year following their initial church membership, and then compared that to the number of friends that church dropouts had made in their first year. The study found that those who remained active made an average of seven good friends; those who dropped out made fewer than two.[6]

The growth of relationships in a group has been studied by specialists for many years. Mark Knapp and Anita Vangelisti suggest that relationships among group members go through certain stages from first meeting to deep intimacy.[7] Not all relationships, obviously, grow to the most intimate level. But understanding relational development can be helpful for ministry coaches and ministry leaders. Here's a brief summary of their interesting observations. You can readily see the application to people who come together in a new ministry gathering.

The first stage in Knapp and Vangelisti's model is the initiating stage. This is when people first meet each other and assess their compatibility and comfort with each other. In this stage, people work hard to present themselves as likeable and interesting. They tend to select their words carefully and are reserved in their exposure of more personal issues.

The second stage is the experimenting stage. Here individuals ask questions in order to gain information and attempt to reduce their uncertainty about each other. In this stage, most individuals expect the others in the group to be upbeat and positive, to exhibit appropriate dress and hygiene, and to be courteous. If not enough persons in the group meet those expectations, participants will often decide not to spend any more time in the gathering.

When a sense of comfort and trust has begun to develop in a group, members move on to the intensifying stage. In this stage, they disclose increasingly personal information about themselves. The group develops routines, identity, jargon, and traditions. Members often use the word *we* to describe the group. Conversations have fewer formalities and are continued from previous meetings. Greater empathy develops among group members as the concern of one becomes the concern of the whole. It becomes increasingly difficult for newcomers to become part of the group in this and the next stage.

The fourth stage is called the integrating stage. This is when participants' identities become, in part, associated with the group; participants define themselves as members of the group. They come to value what they share in common—attitudes, interests, and concerns. The group and individual members spend discretionary time together.

The development of relationships in the new ministry is very important. The ministry coach should encourage the leaders to include activities in their gatherings that will purposefully nurture and grow such relationships. As I mentioned, over time participants will experience a change in why they actually participate in the group. Their motivation will move from wanting to learn about a topic or participate in an activity, to eventually wanting to spend time with friends where they feel valued and loved. When that transition occurs, members' commitment to the group strengthens considerably and their participation becomes an increasingly important part of their life.

Leader Training. As new ministries begin to develop in your church, the ministry coach should gather leaders of those ministries together at least once a quarter for communication, updates, and review. These meetings should be focused on one or more of the following six characteristics of a healthy group:

- Spiritual growth: God's love, when experienced, is irresistible.
- Service opportunities: Learning from Christ means learning to give.
- Outreach to others: In the long run, eternity is a long time.

- Meaningful friendships: Few people experience the real joy of being loved.
- Intellectual growth: Faith does not cancel out understanding.
- Fellowship and fun: There's nothing like having a good time together.

The ministry coach should encourage planning teams to integrate each of these six areas into their planning for the new ministry. While each component need not be addressed in each meeting, these characteristics should serve as an overarching guide for navigating the long-term journey of every side door ministry.

Communicate with the Pastor and Other Church Leaders

We have looked at two general areas of responsibility for the ministry coach: identifying passions in the members of the church and supporting those visionaries who are involved in starting a new ministry. The third area is equally important: communicating with key people in the church.

Most marriage counselors agree that communication is the key to a successful relationship. It is also a key to a successful side door strategy in your church. There are two aspects of the ministry coach's communication responsibilities.

Communicate with the Pastor. The ministry coach should schedule a monthly face-to-face update with the pastor. The agenda should include a briefing on such things as:

- How church members have been alerted to the opportunity of starting a new ministry in the past month;
- Who has shown interest in starting a new ministry, and in what area;

- The number of talking-points interviews conducted, and with whom; and
- The progress of new ministries recently started.

Communicate with Church Leaders. The ministry coach should ask all church leaders to be sensitive to major events in the lives of the people in their network. An unexpected medical or financial condition, a new family member, or a special hobby can often be seeds for a new side door ministry if people are given just a little encouragement and direction.

The ministry coach should also be in touch with church leaders when a new ministry initiative is being considered. Organizational structures, boards, and committees in the church should be informed earlier rather than later. Lyle Schaller makes an interesting recommendation as to how the new ministry should be introduced to a church board. He says to present the idea "as an announcement rather than a request. Then follow the announcement with: 'unless, of course, the board objects.'"[8]

If a new ministry idea looks as if it might interface with an existing ministry area in the church, the ministry coach should network with all parties who might be affected. It would be wise to call a meeting with all those involved in order to discuss and share plans. Ask for suggestions on how existing ministries might support and even enhance the new ministry initiative, and vice versa. Connecting people early will create allies and increase the likelihood of ministries and people supporting each other.

Avoiding Problems with Your New Side Doors

Several years ago an article appeared in an online newspaper, with the headline: "If Only a Map Existed . . . Nazi Mines Stop Egypt's Oil Flow."[1] Egypt, it turns out, is the second most heavily land-mined country in the world (after Afghanistan), due to the deadly legacy of World War II German general, Erwin Rommel. Allied troops battled Rommel throughout North Africa between 1940 and 1943. In his retreat, Rommel left millions of land mines beneath the sandy surface, waiting to cause havoc. Besides the thousands of lives that have since been lost, the mines now make inaccessible natural resources of nearly a billion cubic meters of underground water, almost five million barrels of oil, and thirteen trillion cubic feet of natural gas. But only three million of the estimated twenty million mines have been found and cleared. Referring to the dramatic potential development of the country that might occur if its resources could be tapped, the Egyptian president said, "If only a map existed to show us the mines . . ."

When a church harnesses its natural resources of interests, experiences, and passions, it will tap into a powerful development tool for new ministry and outreach. But there are land mines that can frustrate a church's best intentions. In this chapter, I would like to share with you a "map" of some of the most dangerous potential problems you might encounter as your church starts on the journey of building side door ministries.

The Mines and the Map

This map will help your church to avoid some of the land mines that can keep you from tapping the rich human resources God has put just beneath the surface in your congregation.

Land Mine 1: An Unknown Person Wants to Start a New Ministry

If you are in a church of several hundred people or more, there will probably (and hopefully) be some people interested in starting a new ministry who have not had a previous leadership role in your church. This, of course, is no reason to discourage a person from reflecting on his or her passion and considering a new ministry through the church. Every current leader was new and untested at one time.

In this case, consider looking for a coleader for the proposed ministry who has both leadership experience and a passion for the ministry idea. Shared leadership can be a very positive dynamic in any case, assuming the leaders' personalities are compatible. It halves the load and doubles the power. In fact, the benefits of shared leadership are so great that it is reasonable to explore coleadership with anyone who has a vision for a new ministry.

It's a good idea to do some research on any unknown person before the talking-points interview. Check with the leader of any class or small group in which the person participates. Run an online background check. See if the person has an account on a social networking site and learn what you can from that. Remember, all church-sponsored activities assume liability risks. Be confident in the people who will be representing you.

I was talking recently with Brian Uyeda who was for several years the director of lay ministry at Saddleback Church. The congregation at Saddleback has more than twenty thousand people on an average weekend, with more than 60 percent of these people involved in a ministry activity at some time during the year. The church encourages members to come forward with ideas for a new ministry, and most of their hundreds of creative ministries have grown out of a church members' passion. I asked Bryan how, with so many people, the church screens individuals as prospects for starting a new ministry. "We usually have several of our staff in the meeting and can tell pretty quickly whether we're likely to have problems," he told me. Whether your church numbers twenty thousand or twenty, it is important to be diligent in screening future representatives. Remember that your new ministry will come into contact with a number of unchurched people in your community. You want every contact to be positive.

Land Mine 2: You're Skeptical That the Visionary Has the Leadership Skills for Success

Not everyone has the leadership ability, administrative wherewithal, or even the social skills to turn a dream into a reality. But then not every part of the body can throw a rock, smell a rose, or hear a spoken word. So do you do with an enthusiastic visionary when your intuition tells you a ministry is not likely to fly under his or her direction?

The pastor or church ministry coach should ask the following three questions:

1. Does the person's idea itself have merit? If the answer is no, then you probably have both the wrong idea and the wrong person, and you should gracefully move on. If the answer is yes, ask the second question.

2. Are we certain of our assessment about the person? Don't be too quick to write off a person's ability to get things done. There's something a little different about starting a ministry based on passion. Passion can tap into a person's hidden energy cache, which is something that does not always happen in traditional lay ministry. The person may not have done very well on a previous task, but it may also be true that he or she was not motivated, gifted, or knowledgeable in that particular area. However, if you still feel the person lacks the skills to get the new ministry off the ground, go to the third question.

3. Is there someone in our church who might also have an interest in this ministry idea and could fill the leadership void? Actually, there is a good chance the person with the visionary idea will be quite happy to surrender the leadership responsibilities to someone more likely to see the dream realized. Most of us don't like doing what we know we're not good at. So don't assume the person with the idea feels that he or she needs to be in charge. Hopefully, passion is more important to them than power. If not, it's a good sign the whole idea should be nixed.

If the answer to question 3 is not immediately clear, next steps should be discussed about finding a leader. The goal is to find one or more people in the church willing to oversee the start-up of the new ministry. Rick Warren shares Saddleback's approach to this occasional leadership dilemma: "Sometimes a person will have a great idea for ministry but personally doesn't have the leadership skills to pull it off. In that case, it's important to pray that God will raise up a leader who can take the ball and run with it. But if you spend all your time telling people what won't work, they'll eventually stop trying altogether."[2]

If your church has a spiritual gifts discovery process, start the search for a leader among those people who have been identified as having the gift of leadership. It could be a match made in heaven to have a visionary with a passion but who lacks leadership skills working together with a gifted leader who has had no place to use his or her gift. If the ministry coach finds a good prospective leader, and that person is interested in learning more about the new ministry idea, schedule a meeting and bring the visionary and the prospective leader together.

If a potential leader cannot be identified, the ministry coach and the visionary should agree to put the idea on hold until a leader is forthcoming. Think twice (even three times) about giving a green light to someone who is leadership-challenged. I can't say it too often: This person will be representing your church.

Land Mine 3: The Visionary Is Unable to Recruit a Ministry Planning Team

After the talking-points interview, the next step is for the visionary to recruit a ministry planning team and a prayer support team (see chapter 5). It shouldn't be hard for the visionary to find people who agree to pray for the endeavor. After all, who's going to say, "No, I won't pray for you"? But recruiting people who are willing to spend the next year planning and working on this project will be more challenging. Serving on a ministry planning team will require a commitment that not everyone will be ready to make. But remember my earlier recommendation: Because a ministry planning team is so important to successfully starting a new ministry, if three to five people cannot be recruited, the process should be halted until such a team can be found.

There may be different reasons why a visionary has trouble recruiting a team. Here are the most common, along with some suggestions.

Reason 1: The Visionary Doesn't Have the Contacts. The visionary can look for prospective planning team members among friends and relatives, as well as others in the church who are passionate about the issue. However, if your church attendance is over two hundred, chances are good that one person will not know all the passions, interests, and concerns of every member. In this case, the ministry coach can be a catalyst to help bring people in the church together who share similar interests. Network with other staff and lay leaders about people who might be interested in the proposed ministry. Place a notice in the bulletin or make an announcement during the worship service, such as: "There has been some casual discussion about the idea of beginning a new ministry in the area of _____. If you have an interest in this ministry and would like to share your thoughts with us, please join us for a short meeting after the service."

Remember that not every member of the ministry planning team must be a church member. In fact, it may be beneficial if one or two people on the planning team are not involved in the church. Lyle Schaller agrees: "Enlist volunteers who will help create multiple entry paths for new people. Include prospective people in these efforts. Most prospective members prefer to help pioneer a new venture rather than to join an old."[3] Involving nonmembers will freshen up the group and bring new ideas for getting things done. One thing it will certainly do: build friendships between members and nonmembers as they work together on the project. With this approach, one goal for the new ministry is already in the process of being accomplished.

Reason 2: The Vision Isn't Compelling. The visionary may have trouble recruiting a ministry planning team because the vision, or at least the communication of the vision, is not compelling to others. To deal with this before it is a problem, the ministry coach can help the visionary answer the question: What will this ministry look like five years from today if it lived up to God's expectations? Clearly describing the "promised land" to others is the best way to enlist people to begin the journey (see Num. 14:7–8). When the visionary can see, feel, and touch the dream, then sharing it with others will make the vision much more compelling.

However, the person may have trouble finding people who catch his or her vision because no one else has that same vision. This doesn't necessarily mean that the vision should be abandoned. Sometimes it takes a vision pioneer to tenaciously call people to a place beyond their current circumstances. A United Methodist church in Snellville, Georgia, developed a wonderful cancer care ministry that grew out of one woman's initial vision. No one else in the church had perceived the need for, or conceived of, a ministry of this kind. But when this woman was given an opportunity to describe to the church the need and the dream, she had no trouble finding volunteers.

If the visionary cannot recruit a ministry planning team, but he or she is still given the go-ahead to proceed with the new ministry, the ministry coach will most likely be required to spend considerably more time helping in the start-up of this particular ministry. And the odds of the new ministry being successful with only one person pursuing the dream go down significantly.

Reason 3: No One Wants to Work with the Visionary.
If you suspect the reason the visionary cannot recruit a ministry planning team lies in that person's social skills (or lack thereof), face the fact that it is probably time to cut bait. (That's a fishing expression I learned from my brother-in-law. I believe it means to pack things up and call it a day.) It may be God's way of saying, "Not now."

Land Mine 4: The Ministry Planning Team Runs Out of Steam Before It Starts

This problem usually arises because the planning team members lack a clear sense of direction or are not making enough progress to sustain enthusiasm. The Side Door Planning Guide provides specific steps and resources for starting a new ministry. If the leader and the planning team follow the sequence in this guide, they should make good progress. Encourage the leader to follow the process as much as possible. If the ministry planning team is lagging, the ministry coach should check to see what steps the team has completed and, perhaps, what steps it has skipped.

Stay in regular communication with the planning team leader. The leader is encouraged to meet with the ministry coach at least four times: (1) after he or she has filled out the Talking-Points Discussion Guide (appendix H), (2) after the ministry planning team has researched other ministries, (3) after the planning team has clearly defined its target group, and (4) when the team has completed the Ministry Planning Chart (appendix E) for the new ministry. Depending on the ministry planning team, it may be wise to schedule more-frequent meetings or briefings on the team's progress. These are important times for everyone involved in the new ministry, so it's good to keep in touch with each other.

Land Mine 5: The First Meeting of the New Ministry Is a Bust

If the attendance at the first gathering of the new ministry is one that everyone would prefer to forget, it is due to one of two reasons: either people didn't know about the meeting, or people did know about the meeting.

If they didn't know about it, the problem was publicity. There is a helpful chapter in the Side Door Planning Guide on this topic. If the ministry planning team follows the publicity guidelines outlined there, the chances are good that people will know about the ministry's first meeting.

Publicity ideas and materials are often available through national organizations that specialize in a particular area. West Conroe Baptist Church (Conroe, Texas) often has as many as 120 people from the church and the community playing basketball together each week. "This ministry began as a passion of one of our members," says John Moody. The church's ministry partners with Upward Sports (www.upward.org), the world's largest Christian sports league for youth athletics.[4] Want to start a divorce-recovery ministry? Go to www.divorcecare.com. Passionate about starting a community garden ministry? See www.growingpower.org. In many cases you can freely use the existing work of these ministries' professional designers and marketers to publicize your own ministry.

However, even professional marketing agencies are constantly learning how to do their job better. So review the way you advertised the first meeting. Review the wording of the communication, the method of invitation, the timing, and the exposure to the target audience. Evaluate how much effort the planning team put into mass invitations versus personal invitations.

On the other hand, if people in the target audience *did* know about your event, then your problem was not publicity, but perceived value. Those who knew about the event and chose not to attend were saying—by their absence—that the hassle of going was not worth the benefit they thought they would receive. That is, the risk was not worth the reward. But don't be discouraged about no-shows. Use their absence to figure out why people chose not to come. The planning team should ask such questions as: Did we present a benefit that was attractive to our target group? Or, did we only present what we *thought* would be an attractive benefit?

As church folks, we often presume that we know more about how unchurched people think than we really do. We develop our outreach and promotion plans based on our perceptions. More often than not, however, we really don't understand how people in our target group are thinking, nor do we know the hot buttons that motivate them to act. We don't know how to extend an invitation that "sells the sizzle" and makes the promise worth the price. That is why the Side Door Planning Guide provides comprehensive guidelines for conducting focus groups in order to "get into the heads" of the target group. If the planning team did not conduct focus groups with the target audience, this lack of information is most likely the reason for the poor attendance.

But whatever the reason, if your first meeting was a bomb, the question is: Now what?

Gather the planning team together for a debriefing. Begin with prayer, and be honest before God in expressing feelings and desires. Then use the following questions to guide the discussion:

- Was the disappointing turnout a publicity problem or a perceived value problem?
- Should we try the event again? If so, what will we do differently? How certain are we that the results of our next try will be successful?

- If the problem was one of perceived value, we must have misread our target audience. How can we be certain that we understand the real issues our target group is facing? Ask the question that Prince of Peace Lutheran Church (Burnsville, Minnesota) asks the prospective attendees of their new groups: What kind of group would you change your schedule to attend?
- Should we conduct focus groups to be sure that we understand the mind-set of our target audience? Businesses and marketing companies often do this when it appears that their marketing strategy needs to go back to the drawing board.

If the planning team decides to try again, it is important that their best effort is put into it. If the second attempt is also a bomb, the ministry dream is, for all practical purposes, dead.

Land Mine 6: Subsequent Gatherings Are Flagging in Attendance and Enthusiasm

One nice thing about a new group or activity is that it can handle rapid change. If fewer and fewer people are attending the events, participants are concluding that the benefit is not worth the cost, and changes need to be made. If people don't seem to resonate with where the ministry is going, here are some evaluative questions to ask:

- Have we clearly and specifically defined our target audience? Remember, the more specifically the target audience is defined, the more likely people's individual interests and needs can be identified and addressed.

- Have we accurately identified the most significant felt needs of our target audience? Remember, it's not what we think is important, it's what they feel is important.
- Did we focus on, and meet, those felt needs? An effective ministry will eventually meet three needs, in this order: felt needs, deeper needs, and eternal needs. But if the ministry does not meet the first level of need, people won't be around for you to meet the second or third.
- Did prospective participants know about upcoming gatherings? As I mentioned, your problem may simply be one of communication. Don't pass out a monthly calendar with the time and the dates of the meetings and then expect people to remember the information. Send e-mails, make phone calls, send postcards. Redundancy is the most reliable form of communication.
- Has there been enough time to conclude that the ministry actually has a declining trend? It is common to see declining attendance for the first three to four meetings and then see it pick up. Be sure there is a clear pattern of low return rate and not just normal attrition. Since attrition is normal in the first several meetings, do everything possible to start out with a critical mass of people that can weather this anticipated drop off.
- Were absentees followed up? Sometimes the "back door" that people slip through can be closed simply by letting them know they were missed. Send a card or e-mail with a personal note to anyone who attended but did not return. Mention that their presence is appreciated and you hope they can come again. Below is a simple anonymous survey that may help reconnect with these individuals.

Our goal in the new _____ group is to connect people with a common interest in _____. We've had several gatherings over the past few months and are learning a lot. We would like to see this group move to the next level and be even more helpful to those who are involved. If you would take a moment to answer a few questions, it will help us plan for the future. Thank you. (Note the enclosed stamped envelope. Also, providing your name for question 4 is optional.)

1. How many events of the _____ group have you attended?

2. To what extent did you find these events to be helpful? (Circle one)
   Very much   Mostly   A little   Not at all

3. What would you suggest to make this gathering more helpful or enjoyable?

4. If you would be interested in sharing some time and ideas to help make this group even better, please write your name and contact information below.

- Is there a sense of ownership among attendees? The best way to develop commitment to a group is for participants to have a part in the group's direction. Ask those in attendance to help identify important topics and plan future meetings. This will improve the quality of the meetings as well as enlarge the number of people who have a stake in its success.

There may be other reasons causing poor or declining participation: Is the gathering at an inconvenient day, time, or location? Is the meeting too long or too short? Is child care necessary? Is the person in charge effective at facilitating group dynamics? Don't wait too long to reassess if your attendance is trending downward.

Land Mine 7: The Gathering Does Not Have Any Unchurched Participants

This situation requires immediate attention. If the people attending these new ministry events are all church members, it will be increasingly difficult for unchurched people to get involved. Having unchurched people in your new ministry from day one is so important that if the gathering does not have at least 25 percent nonmembers after the first three meetings, I believe further meetings should be suspended until a plan can be developed to address the problem.

Why might no unchurched people be involved? Let's look at some likely reasons.

They Weren't Personally Invited. The positive response to personal invitations from a friend or relative (via e-mail, phone call, face-to-face invitation, etc.) will be about 25 percent to 30 percent. The response to mass-media invitations (bulk mailings, newspaper ads, posters, etc.) will be less than 1 percent. Often, churches invite their own members through personal invitation, but then invite nonmembers only by mailing brochures. Use the social networks of members to personally invite nonmember friends and relatives.

They See the Gathering as Too Religious. While you're not trying to hide who you are, these gatherings are primarily a time to come together around what every attendee has in common. Not everyone shares the experience of attending church. Remember, start with everyone's felt needs.

They Are Reticent to Meet at a Church Facility. Most unchurched people feel somewhat awkward entering a church building. How would you feel attending a meeting in a Mormon temple or a Hindu shrine? Consider a partnership with a local organization or business whose focus complements the new ministry. A hospital, hobby shop, preschool, retirement home, restaurant, etc. could be happy to host the group and even help publicize the activities. This by itself will go a long way toward increasing the number of unchurched people who will attend your meetings.

Land Mine 8: Meaningful Relationships Are Not Developing among Participants

Building relationships among participants in your new ministry will be an essential part of its success. Good icebreaker activities help people learn about each other. When we share with others about our personal backgrounds, likes and dislikes, families, jobs, fears, and joys, it lets people into a more intimate understanding of who we are. What makes you happy? Anxious? What was your childhood like? These are questions that will build empathy and trust.

Or, try eating together. Something special happens when we share a meal with others. It creates a comfortable environment in which to relax, laugh, share, and bond. John Chandler, a long-time student of effective churches, observes, "Not all clusters [groups] that grow eat together, but all clusters that do eat together seem to grow. . . . It is our overwhelming experience that eating together is one of the best ways to build community."[5]

Participants should be encouraged to share special events in each other's lives: graduations, new babies, illnesses, job promotions or losses, health concerns, engagements, and grandchildren. If someone's family member is sick or struggling, group prayer (or even just prayer from the leader) will be much appreciated. These gatherings are a great opportunity for celebrating victories and sharing sorrows. Any big event to an individual, should be a big event to the group.

Providing support is not something only Christians can do; anyone can empathize and encourage another. This happens all the time in non-Christian circles. But adding Christian empathy and prayer to a situation provides a unique experience of Christian faith, hope, and love to those who are not yet believers. One of the great values of a side door group is that it gives participants in the group relationships with fellow travelers to share some of life's journey. The oft-quoted phrase is true: People don't care how much you know until they know how much you care.

Every new ministry, at some point within the first year, should grow beyond meeting felt needs and include providing for deeper needs. Felt needs, of course, are not insignificant. A single mom with three kids has immediate felt needs concerning her time, health, finances, and emotions. Those needs are certainly real and pressing. But after people's felt needs are met, the deeper needs of their souls still yearn for solace. "The difference between real and felt needs is important to understand," note Harvie Conn and Manuel Ortiz. "The felt needs of poor people often deal with the physical—food, housing, transportation, medicine. However, the deeper, real need has to do with valuing themselves as creations of God, reclaiming the dignity God desires them to have, and finding the hope of a transformed life in Christ."[6]

What are people's deeper needs? As we saw earlier, people are looking for a place to belong and a sense of balance. They are seeking authentic relationships and spiritual answers to their questions. People want help through life's tough transitions.

Addressing people's deeper needs should be a long-term purpose of all special-interest ministries, regardless of the original felt need they gathered around. As participants can grow to become sensitive to, and then respond to, these deeper needs, bonding occurs in a powerful way, regardless of whether group members are Christians or non-Christians.

In the book *Who Cares about Love?* I suggest five guidelines for deepening relationships.[7] Ministry leaders can teach about these and other principles in group gatherings:

- Learn and practice the skills of listening.
- Deepen your level of communication with others.
- Practice empathy.
- Identify needs in people's lives.
- Respond to people's needs with an appropriate, caring gift.

Deeper needs are more naturally identified in a support-type ministry than a recreationally oriented ministry. But in either case, time spent responding to deeper needs will cause deeper relationships to grow.

Land Mine 9: Church Members Do Not Bond with Unchurched Group Members

Be conscious of the social dynamics when the group is together. Do church members and nonmembers seem comfortable with each other? Are they enjoying each other's company, or do church members seem to cluster with other church friends and ignore the nonmembers?

If you see social segregation happening, group leaders should speak privately with the church people about it. Remind them that there are nonmembers in the group and that it is important for them to go out of their way to involve everyone in conversation and activities. In icebreakers, projects, and other group activities, intentionally pair members and nonmembers together. Encourage church members to invite nonmembers to extracurricular activities and to go out of their way to extend Christian hospitality to them.

Land Mine 10: Unchurched People in the New Ministry Do Not Come to Church

If your church has only one worship service, and the service has not changed much over the past forty years, ask yourself whether an unchurched person would really feel comfortable there. In many churches across America, the services are honestly not very appealing to unchurched people. (Why do you think they don't come in the first place?) The in-house language, the welcome (or lack thereof), and the quality and content of the services are just not attractive to people who aren't used to going to church.

Of course, most church services are not designed for the unchurched, and that's fine. I'm not suggesting you change the entire format and focus of your worship service for the benefit of a small minority of unchurched people. So what's my point?

In the first twelve months of your relationship with unchurched people through the new ministry, it is not necessary that they be in your Sunday morning service. Of course, there is certainly nothing wrong with them showing up. And if they do come, they should be warmly welcomed. A friend from the ministry group should sit with them, introduce them to the pastor and to friends in the church, and even invite them out to dinner after the service. But the process of coming to faith is one that takes time. It is likely that attending a Sunday worship service, while important, will come later in their progress rather than earlier.

Big events at a church provide great opportunities for bringing new friends from the group, as do Christmas concerts, summer outings, and mission trips. Most unchurched people participating in a new ministry will not go to a church-sponsored event if they aren't personally invited. But many will go if they are invited. I was in Little Rock, Arkansas, where First Baptist Church had just finished their first HuntFest. The church is not extremely large by today's standards, 450 or so. But one of the members had come up with the idea of a six-hour gathering for hunters and their families. At this gathering, they had kids' activities, a great meal, and door prizes (including a new all-terrain vehicle). They sold more than eleven hundred tickets (at twenty dollars each), and 75 percent of those tickets went to unchurched friends, family, and community members. The HuntFest provided church members with a perfect opportunity to invite unchurched friends.

If you don't have the wherewithal to put on big events, there may be Christian events going on in the community. Perhaps a larger church or ministry is putting on a concert. A popular Christian speaker or author may be giving a talk across town. Even if you have to drive an hour or stay somewhere overnight, events like this provide great ways to strengthen relationships and provide people with additional exposure to the Christian message.

Land Mine 11: People Do Not Come to Christian Faith

"Once you have created a new side door into your church," says Todd Pridemore, "it is important to think about how to most appropriately invite non-church members involved in that activity to consider becoming disciples of Jesus. Side doors are often just the first of many steps in the process of making disciples."[8]

The graphic below reminds us of the three kinds of needs we have mentioned which an effective special-interest ministry should ultimately address. This does not mean that when a group moves from one level to the next that they should abandon the previous one. It means that over time the group should be meeting all three kinds of needs.

time

George Hunter alludes to these three distinct issues in his book, *The Apostolic Congregation*: "First, get in ministry with pre-Christian people, then get in conversation with them, then include God in the conversation."[9]

In the ultimate scheme of things, your church is eventually all about a personal faith in, and relationship with, Jesus Christ. Side door ministries should introduce people to the joy of life in Christ and in the body of Christ. As people outside the church develop meaningful connections with Christians, those friendships become the bridges of God for many people to experience God's love firsthand. "I've never been able to persuade someone intellectually to abandon the relativistic mind-set," says Daniel Hill, on staff at Willow Creek's Axis ministry. "What's more likely to happen is that they'll see the power of a transformed life in another Christ follower and be transformed."[10]

One of the great benefits of a side door is that it provides a place where non-Christians can develop genuine and unconditional friendships with Christians. And the feeling is mutual. "Because compassion is core to our purpose," says Nathan Oates of Emmaus Church Community, "we will seek to be a church community that goes to the people. We will reach people by loving people." Oates further says, "Individual transformation will fuel, and be fueled by, authentic expressions of Christian community."[11]

This does not mean that we simply hope Jesus oozes out of the pores of church members and sticks to the nonmembers. It means that the ministry planning team, with the encouragement from the pastor and the ministry coach, should seek to create an environment that is spiritually conducive for God's love to flow through the relationships in the group. The following are a few thoughts for creating such a spiritual environment.

Appoint a Chaplain. Every new ministry, regardless of its purpose, should have a chaplain. This person brings a relevant devotional thought and a prayer at each gathering; circulates and delivers get-well cards to anyone in the group who is sick; and prays for, sends flowers to, or visits ministry participants (and even their family members) who may be in special need. The chaplain's purpose is to bring a spiritual ethos to the group and its activities.

Provide Times of Spiritual Exposure. Each gathering of the new ministry should have a time during which members are exposed (if even just briefly) to spiritual matters. Perhaps it is through a short devotional by the chaplain or group leader. Maybe it is through a story or a news article from the Internet that has a spiritual perspective. It might be through a reference to something at church the past week or in a sermon series. "Communication theorists partly explain attitude change and conversion by the 'cumulative effect' of many communications and experiences over time," writes George Hunter. "Willow Creek Community Church confirmed the theory and popularized the analogy of the 'chain of experiences.' Each experience adds a link in the chain that leads to faith and new life."[12]

Create a Spiritual Culture. A few years ago, I saw an article in the *Colorado Springs Gazette*, a local community newspaper, reporting on over 250 side door sports and recreation ministries of First Presbyterian Church. The following paragraph jumped out at me: "Every event builds in a faith component. . . . More than thirty-nine thousand people participate in First Presbyterian's recreational [side door] ministries every year; about 40 percent come from outside the church. Church leaders want that percentage to go up. The ideal split, they say, is about fifty-fifty, which allows unchurched folks to easily meet and form friendships with churchgoers. Those friendships create a base for spiritual growth."[13]

Pray. Everyone has needs and concerns. According to research, 81 percent of Americans pray.[14] It is quite appropriate for the group's chaplain to ask members if they, or anyone they know, would like prayer. Anyone in the group may pray, but no one should feel uncomfortable if they don't want to. It has been my experience that non-Christians are more likely to ask for prayer for friends or family than for themselves. And I believe that God hears and answers the prayers of non-Christians.

James Engel has developed a helpful visualization of how and when people come to Christian faith, known as the Engel Scale.[15] This scale illustrates that conversion is really more of a process than an event and that people progress through various stages in their faith pilgrimage. Bob Whitesel has written an excellent book, *Spiritual Waypoints*, which further applies the Engel Scale in the faith journey.[16]

Level	Description
-11	No God framework
-10	Experience of emptiness
-9	Vague awareness of and belief in God
-8	Wondering if God can be known
-7	Aware of Jesus
-6	Interested in Jesus
-5	Experience of Christian love
-4	Aware of the basic facts of the gospel
-3	Aware of personal need
-2	Grasp the implications of the gospel
-1	Challenged to respond personally
0	Repentance and faith
+1	Post-decision evaluation
+2	Functioning member of local church
+3	Conceptual and behavioral growth

One important point that Engle's scale helps us to see is the fact that people progress through steps in their Christian pilgrimage, and that not every unbeliever in a side door gathering will be at the same place. Engel makes the important point that effective evangelism means helping people move forward one step at a time. It is a mistake (and studies show it is actually counterproductive) to expect people to jump straight to repentance and faith, regardless of where they may be on the scale.[17]

Over the course of a non-Christian's movement toward repentance and faith, conversations will touch on Christ and Christianity. "Loving acts and compassion are foundational to our witness," says Rebecca Pippert. "But if we never share the reason for our love, we run the risk of non-believers thinking we're simply Boy Scouts. As important as love is—it's not enough."[18] Scripture tells us, "Always be prepared to give an answer to everyone who asks you to give the reason for the hope that you have. But do this with gentleness and respect" (1 Pet. 3:15). So what does a Christian say to an unbeliever when the topic of religion comes up?

Four Helpful Questions

I have found the following four questions to be helpful in spiritual conversations. These questions—and their answers—could be the basis for a series of sermons, classes, or small group studies in your church. Then, when the subject of faith arises with an unbeliever, church members will have already thought about their answers.

- How has being a Christian made a difference in my life?
- What does it mean to be a Christian (using words understandable to a non-Christian)?
- Why would I like my friend to be a Christian and a member of my church?
- How does a person become a Christian (using words understandable to a non-Christian)?

Conclusion

I hope this chapter has not discouraged you from seeing the powerful possibilities of side doors in your church. Realistic leaders know that a worthwhile task or journey will not be without its challenges. My purpose in this chapter has been to help you anticipate difficult scenarios and be prepared before they come up.

While there will certainly be obstacles, the joy of helping Christians pursue their passion through new ministries is one of the most fulfilling things to be experienced in the equipping ministry.

On Beyond Zebra

One of the most popular titles of the revered children's author Dr. Seuss is his book *On Beyond Zebra*. If you have not read this imaginative classic, *On Beyond Zebra* introduces us to amazing new letters we never thought might exist beyond our familiar twenty-six-letter alphabet. But letters such as "Yuzz," "Wum," "Humpf," "Fuddle," and "Glikk" stretch our thoughts to all kinds of creative possibilities. His book comes to my mind here because there are also amazing possibilities we never thought might exist beyond the now familiar idea of side door ministries. But unlike the imaginary stories of Dr. Seuss, the stories and ideas in this final chapter have a solid basis in reality—they are actually happening. The special-interest ministries in some churches have grown into amazing and exciting possibilities on beyond zebra.

A Signature Ministry

In some churches, what began as a group of people sharing a common interest or concern has grown beyond participants' wildest imagination. Beginning with a small gathering of passionate people, these ministries have mushroomed into "signature ministries"—activities that have developed into high visibility ministries that influence a substantial number of people in their communities.

"A signature ministry," Reverend L. D. Wood-Hull told his members at St. Barnabas Episcopal Church (Portland, Oregon) "is when someone in our neighborhood discovers you belong to St. Barnabas, and says, 'Oh, St. Barnabas—you're the ones who [fill in signature ministry here].'"[1]

A signature ministry is often an umbrella of activities and services that are widely known in the community and define a significant part of the church's public identity. In some cases, these ministries actually become independent, non-profit 501(c)(3) organizations with their own officers, budget, and facility. Then it really gets exciting.

The motorcycle ministry at Grove City Church of the Nazarene (Columbus, Ohio) began when a few young men started getting together after church for a ride. It grew to become an independent organization with its own name (Gears) that sponsored a variety of special events and community service projects. The annual Biker Weekend of this church's signature ministry is now the largest gathering of motorcyclists in the state of Ohio.

The cancer ministry of Cannon United Methodist Church (Snellville, Georgia) began in the heart of one member who had lost a good friend to breast cancer. The experience motivated her into action, and today the services of this signature ministry include client visitation, prayer teams, chemo buddies, child care, transportation, financial counseling, and meal provision. The ministry has spread Christlike love to more than one thousand families since its inception.

The Washington Cathedral (Redmond, Washington) has spawned five different nonprofit signature ministries since its birth in 1984, each of which grew from the passion of just a few people in the church. These signature ministries include Together for Transformation, which focuses on empowering those most hurting in the church's community; the Health Resource Center, which sponsors twelve-step ministries, a counseling center, and medical clinics; EXCEL Business Ministries, which helps people discover that success in the marketplace is fulfilling God's plan for their lives on an ethical pathway; Washington Seminary, which offers four state-approved master's degrees and includes four different schools training Christians for excellence in lay ministry; and Build the Family Center, which specializes in working to make the world a safer place for children.

Affinity Churches, House Churches, and Beyond

Some of the new ministries that are started in your church may even grow to become churches themselves. In fact, if your church presently offers only one service, on only one day of the week, at only one time of day, with only one style of music that attracts only one type of worshiper, then it might well be appropriate to actually encourage some of your stronger side door ministries to become new churches. Ginghamsburg United Methodist Church near Dayton, Ohio, has, at last count, twenty-three different specialized churches under its ministry umbrella.

House churches are growing rapidly across the country as places that provide a genuine source of Christian caring and community. Some of your new ministries may develop real momentum of unity and community, and attract many who would feel out of place in your existing church. If so, consider giving birth to a daughter church.

Perhaps an affinity church is in the future of some of your new ministries. Take the Church in the Wind (Denver, Colorado) that began as an outreach to the motorcycle community and has now expanded to include skateboarders, truckers, veterans, snowbirds, and others. Or the United Methodist Church of the Joyful Healer (McKinleyville, California), a karate church whose ministry has grown dramatically from the original passion of its founder to lose weight and lower his blood pressure. Or the Happy Trails Cowboy Church (Hiddenite, North Carolina) with services every Monday night in a local rodeo arena. (By the way, if anyone in your church has a hankerin' to rope some li'l doggies, there is a national Cowboy Church Network, www.cowboychurch.net, that will be happy to help get you started.)

"When people find somebody with the same passion they have," says Richard Harris of the Southern Baptist Home Mission Board, "they are interested, and attracted."[2] The Southern Baptist denomination started more than seventeen hundred affinity churches in a recent year, including golf churches, bluegrass churches, motorcycle churches, and lots of cowboy churches.

So wherever your side door journey takes you, my friend, I wish you well. There are exciting days ahead for you and your church. I hope the ideas I have shared have given you a sense of optimism as well as encouragement for what God can do in your church—how he can use the unique passions found in your congregation to bring others into his family and into the fellowship of

Christ's church. As you embark on your journey, remember the Old Testament story of Mordecai, a man who was desperately trying to save the Jewish people from destruction. The words he wrote to Queen Esther may well be the words God is speaking to you and to your congregation at this moment: "Who knows whether you have not come to the kingdom for such a time as this?" (Est. 4:14 ESV).

Epilogue

In closing, I would like to share a story from Russell Conwell's classic lecture, "Acres of Diamonds."[1] It can remind us of the marvelous potential for new ministry and outreach hidden just beneath the surface in our congregations. It is also a reminder about how easily we can miss that potential God has given us.

There was once a farmer who lived in the mountains of Africa. He owned a large farm full of orchards, grain fields, and gardens. He was a wealthy, contented man. Contented because he was wealthy, and wealthy because he was contented.

One day a visitor came to his farm and described the fortunes being made by people discovering diamond mines. The visitor spoke in vivid detail of the beautiful stones that looked like drops of "congealed sunlight." He described how a handful of diamonds could purchase any desire of the farmer's heart and could place his children on thrones around the world through the influence of his great wealth.

That night the farmer went to bed a poor man—poor because he was discontented, and discontented because he feared he was poor. As the farmer lay on his bed thinking about wealth, he said aloud, "I want a mine of diamonds." All night he lay awake thinking about diamonds. When morning came, he sought out the stranger for directions to where these gleaming gems might be found.

"In white sands between high mountains," he was told.

"I will go," said the farmer.

So he sold his farm, left his family in a neighbor's care, and went in search of diamonds. He searched through mountains and valleys, deserts and plains. For years he sought to find a mine of diamonds. At last, when his money was spent and his clothes were in rags, he stood wretched and ruined on a bridge, looking down at the swirling water below. That poor, afflicted, suffering man could not resist the awful temptation to cast himself into the depths below, where he sank beneath the dark surface, never to rise again.

Sometime later, the man who had purchased the farm was walking along the stream on his property. He happened to look down, and as he did, he noticed a curious flash of light. The man reached down and picked up a dark-colored stone, having an eye that beautifully reflected the colors of the rainbow. He took the curious stone into his house, left it on the mantle, and thought no more about it.

Months later the same stranger returned. Upon entering the house, he saw the flash of light from the stone on the mantle and rushed over to it.

"This is a diamond," he said. "This is a diamond!"

"No, no," said the owner, "that's not a diamond. It's just a stone I found out in my stream."

"It is a diamond," insisted the stranger.

Together the two returned to the stream and stirred up the white sands with their fingers. There they found other, more beautiful, more valuable gems than the first. Thus was discovered the actual mine of Golconda, the most prolific diamond mine in the history of mankind.

The old farmer had owned acres of diamonds. Every acre—yes, every shovel-full from that old farm—contained the gleaming gems. Yet he had sold his land for practically nothing in order to look for diamonds elsewhere. Had the farmer only taken the time to know what diamonds look like in their rough state, and had he first explored his own land, he would have discovered more riches than he had ever imagined possible right under his own feet.

This compelling true story reminds me of a very real fact: nearly every pastor, at this moment, is standing on his or her own acres of diamonds. Look again at your congregation, now with more educated eyes. Do you see flashes of light in those common stones? Do you see sparkles of value in the passions, the strengths, and the experiences of your people? If you look closely, if you recognize those flashes of passion in their rough state, they are diamonds.

Go ahead. Reach out and pick them up. Break them loose from their self- or church-inflicted limitations, and allow those passions to reflect the Son's light. Hone them. Shape them. Those passions hold the potential to bring more people to the throne of Jesus Christ and into the fellowship of your church than you ever imagined possible.

Appendixes

The contents of these appendixes are available as free and unrestricted reproducible downloads at www.wphresources.com/sidedoor.

Appendix A
Side Door Assessment Chart

Activity	Average attendance in past 6 months	Average unchurched attendance in past 6 months	Percentage of unchurched ([column 3 ÷ 2] x 100)	Side Door? Yes if within 25%–75%
Totals				

Appendix B
New Member Assessment Chart

	Conversion		Transfer		Biological		TOTAL	
	#	%	#	%	#	%	#	%
5 years ago								100%
4 years ago								100%
3 years ago								100%
2 years ago								100%
Last year								100%
TOTAL								100%

Appendix C
Congregational Survey

Thank you for taking a few moments to complete the following survey. The purpose for requesting this information is to develop a "personality profile" of our church family, to identify common ages, interests, concerns, marital status, family status, etc. If you are a member or regular attendee of our church, we would appreciate you taking time to complete and return this survey. As our church profile becomes clearer, we will share the information as we explore ways to be most effective in ministry to and through the body of Christ.

Please complete one survey per person (thirteen years and older).

Born in year: _____

Marital Status

❏ I am presently **single** (please check one box below)

❏ Never married

❏ Divorced; number of years since most recent divorce: _____

❏ Widow(er); number of years since most recent loss: _____

❏ Other: _____

❏ I am presently **married** (please check one box below)

❏ First marriage; number of years married: _____

❏ Second marriage; number of years in present marriage: _____

❏ Third marriage; number of years in present marriage: _____

❏ I am presently **separated**
number of months or years since separation: _____

Family Status (check all that apply)

❏ I have children living at home.
List birth year of each child. _____

❏ I have grandchildren living at home.
List birth year of each child. _____

❏ There are one or more children at home who are not biologically related to me (blended family, adopted, legal custody, foster, etc.).

❏ I have grown children living out of the house.

❏ I have some grown children still at home.
List birth year of each child. _____

_____

❏ I have never had children.

❏ I have minor (biologically related) children who are not living at home.

Special Interests

The hobbies I enjoy and the approximate number of hours I spend with each hobby in an average month:

Hobby	Hours per month
_____	_____
_____	_____
_____	_____
_____	_____

Special Concerns

Beyond what might be considered normal concerns, I feel particularly worried about:

❏ My marriage

❏ My children

❏ My parents

❏ My health

❏ My job

❏ My finances

❏ _____

❏ _____

Life Experiences

I have experienced the following events within the past **five years** (check all that apply).

- ❏ Death of a spouse
- ❏ Divorce
- ❏ Move to nursing/ retirement home
- ❏ Marital separation
- ❏ Death of a close family member
- ❏ Major physical problems
- ❏ Marriage or remarriage
- ❏ Void of personal life goals
- ❏ Financial loss of retirement money
- ❏ Forced early retirement
- ❏ Loss of ability to drive
- ❏ Marital reconciliation
- ❏ Retirement
- ❏ Spouse confined to nursing home
- ❏ Change in health of family member

- ❏ Change in number of arguments with spouse
- ❏ Took out a loan over $300,000
- ❏ Foreclosure on a mortgage/ loan
- ❏ Significant feeling of not being wanted/needed
- ❏ Outstanding personal achievement
- ❏ Spouse began or stopped work
- ❏ Significant decrease in contact with children
- ❏ Dramatic change in personal behavior patterns
- ❏ Significant decrease in contact with friends
- ❏ Trouble with boss/supervisor
- ❏ Minor physical problems
- ❏ Significant change in recreational habits
- ❏ Significant change in church activities
- ❏ Significant change in social activities
- ❏ Took out a loan of less than $300,000

❏ Gain a new family member

❏ Significant change in financial condition

❏ Death of a close friend

❏ Difficulty in getting medical insurance

❏ Significant change in sleep habits

❏ Change in frequency of family get-togethers

❏ Significant change in eating habits

❏ Minor law violation

Appendix D
Model Church Summary

Church Name: _____

Church Address: _____

_____

Church Phone: (_____) _____

Church Website: __www._____

Average Weekend Attendance: _____ Number of Services:_____

Day/Time of Services: _____

Year the Church Started: _____

Denomination: _____

Name of Ministry: _____

Ministry Website: __www._____
(if different from church)

Date of Phone Interview: _____

With: _____

Title: _____

Your Name: _____

How and when did the ministry begin?

Does the ministry have a written purpose statement? (Obtain a copy if possible.)

What kind of activities does the ministry engage in? What comments do you have about these activities?

Ministry Activity	Comments

Are there plans for expanding the ministry? If so, in what ways?

What obstacles or challenges were encountered in the birth or growth of this ministry?

How were they handled?

What suggestions do you have about how to avoid these problems or what to do if they are encountered?

Are you aware of any resources that would be helpful to us in this area?

Books:

Organizations/People:

Websites:

Churches with similar ministries:

Seminars, conferences, etc.:

Do you have any other comments or suggestions that would be helpful to us in starting a similar ministry in our church?

Appendix E
Ministry Planning Chart

	Target Audience	Others Affected
1. Felt need(s) of our target audience		
2. Our goal(s) for responding to people's felt needs		
3. The steps for achieving our goals		

Stage 1: FELT NEEDS

	Target Audience	Others Affected
Stage 2: DEEPER NEEDS 1. Our goal for responding to people's deeper needs	To build increasingly meaningful and caring relationships among those touched by our ministry (both church members and nonmembers).	
2. The steps for achieving our goals		

	Target Audience	Others Affected
Stage 3: ETERNAL NEEDS 1. Our goal for responding to people's eternal needs	To help those affected by our ministry to grow in their understanding and experience of God's love.	
2. The steps for achieving our goals		

Appendix F
Goal Planning Worksheet

Goal:			
Action Steps	**Deadline**	**Person Responsible**	**Cost**
1.	1.	1.	1.
2.	2.	2.	2.
3.	3.	3.	3.
4.	4.	4.	4.

Appendix G
Publicity Planning Worksheet

*Proposed first meeting date:*_____

People to invite to be a part of the publicity planning:			
Publicity Task	**Person Responsible**	**Date to Be Completed**	**Cost**
1.	1.	1.	1.
2.	2.	2.	2.
3.	3.	3.	3.
4.	4.	4.	4.

Appendix H
Talking Points Discussion Guide

Purpose of These Questions

You are reading these pages because you have a heartbeat! Your physical heart, of course, is beating inside your body. But you also have an emotional heart beating inside your soul. It is your priorities, values, and passions that have been growing in you since birth. Your emotional heartbeat is what makes you . . . you.

The following questions will help you consider whether your emotional heartbeat—the passions God has created in you—might be the seed of a new group or ministry that could touch people with God's love—a side door ministry. This brief conversation guide will help you to think through such a possibility, and then organize the discussion in an exploratory interview between you and your pastor or ministry coach.

Prior to the meeting, please think about, and then write out, your responses to the questions below. Bring two copies to the meeting. These questions will help you clarify your thoughts, as well as give others a better likelihood of understanding your ideas, and perhaps even enhancing these ideas for maximum ministry.

What's Your Dream?

In a few sentences, explain what kind of ministry you're thinking about.

Take a moment and envision what this ministry might look like five years from today (such as, how many people are involved or touched by the ministry, what activities are occurring, etc.).

What past experiences (personally or professionally) have you had that qualify you in this area of ministry?

Do you know anyone (church members or otherwise) who might be interested in working with you to pursue this new ministry idea? Who are they and how do you know them?

What Is the Need?

Who would be affected by—and benefit from—this ministry?

What other organizations or churches are you aware of that provide a related service or ministry in our community? In other areas of the city or country?

What Is the Opportunity?

A key part of considering new ministries in our church is the potential for connecting with, and reaching out to, new and unchurched people. How do you see this occurring in this ministry?

What Will It Cost?

What kind of financial requirements and expenses do you anticipate (short-term and long-term)?

Can you think of some ways these expenses might be covered?

Notes

Introduction

1. John Stott, "The Model—Becoming More Like Christ" (sermon, Keswick Convention, Keswick, Cumbria, England, July 17, 2007), http://www.christiantoday.com/article/john.stott.final.sermon.the.model.becoming.more.like.christ/12442.htm.

2. Michael Anthony, "Testing the Research: Do People Still Come Through Relationships?" (presentation to American Society for Church Growth, November 14, 2008, Talbot Seminary, La Mirada, California).

3. Tom Mercer, *8 to 15: The World Is Smaller Than You Think* (Victorville, Calif.: Oikos, 2011), 17.

4. Michael Green, *Evangelism in the Early Church* (Grand Rapids, Mich.: Eerdmans, 1970), 210.

5. Donald McGavran, *Bridges of God: A Study in the Strategy of Missions* (London: World Dominion, 1955).

6. Anthony, "Testing the Research."

7. Win Arn and Charles Arn, *The Master's Plan for Making Disciples: Every Christian an Effective Witness through an Enabling Church* (Grand Rapids, Mich.: Baker, 1998), 81.

8. Donald McGavran, *Understanding Church Growth* (Grand Rapids, Mich.: Eerdmans, 1990), 209.

9. George G. Hunter III, *The Apostolic Congregation: Church Growth Reconceived for a New Generation* (Nashville: Abingdon, 2009), 62.

Chapter 1

1. George G. Hunter III, *The Apostolic Congregation: Church Growth Reconceived for a New Generation* (Nashville: Abingdon, 2009), 62.

2. Todd Pridemore, "Does Your Church Have Side Doors?" *Net Results*, September/October 2004, 6.

3. George G. Hunter III, *To Spread the Power: Church Growth in the Wesleyan Spirit* (Nashville: Abingdon, 1987), 79.

4. Kwasi Kena, "Offering Christ Today: Church Growth—Priority One, Be Fruitful," *Evangelism*, 2005.

5. Hunter, *The Apostolic Congregation*, 115.

6. Lyle Schaller, "How to Attract New People" in "Cultivating Active Church Members," accessed September 17, 2013, http://www.buildingchurchleaders.com/downloads/practical ministryskills/cultivatingactivechurchmembers/, 3.

7. Gary L. McIntosh, *Beyond the First Visit: The Complete Guide to Connecting Guests to Your Church* (Grand Rapids, Mich.: Baker, 2006), 22.

8. "Emergent Dialogue," *Denver Seminary Magazine*, Fall 2004, 5.

9. Alan Roxburgh and Fred Romanuk, *The Missional Leader: Equipping Your Church to Reach a Changing World* (San Francisco: Jossey-Bass, 2006), xv.

10. Hunter, *The Apostolic Congregation*, 116.

11. David Williamson, "Eight Ways to Reach Out to the Community Through Small Groups," accessed September 17, 2013, http://www.sheltonfbc.org/documents/09.28.08LGCoaching Tips.pdf.

12. Hunter, *The Apostolic Congregation*, 115.

13. Lee Sparks, "The State of Volunteer Ministry," *Rev! Magazine*, January/February 2009, 52.

14. Win Arn, "Solving the Problem of Motivation," The Win Arn Growth Report, vol. 25, 2.

15. Hunter, *The Apostolic Congregation*, 62.

16. Donald McGavran, *Understanding Church Growth* (Grand Rapids, Mich.: Eerdmans, 1990), 53.

17. Donald McGavran, "How to Grow a Church," 16mm film (Monrovia, Calif.: Church Growth, 1976).

18. Win Arn and Charles Arn, *The Church Growth Ratio Book* (Monrovia, Calif.: Church Growth, 2002), 26.

19. "Outreach," Center Grove Presbyterian Church, accessed September 17, 2013, http://www.centergrove.org/outreach.htm.

20. Lyle Schaller in "Ask Pastor Lynn" by Lynn Fanfora in "Together" (newsletter of Hope Evangelical Lutheran Church, Citrus Springs, Fla.), June 2007, http://www.hopelc.org/ sermons2007/June%202007%20Together.pdf, 3.

21. Rick Warren, *The Purpose Driven Church: Every Church Is Big in God's Eyes* (Grand Rapids, Mich.: Zondervan, 1995), 326.

22. For more information about the Chicago Lights Urban Farm in the Cabrini-Green neighborhood, go to fourthchurch.org/ chicagolights/urban-farm.html.

23. Ray Bowman, *When Not to Build: An Architect's Unconventional Wisdom for the Growing Church* (Grand Rapids, Mich.: Baker, 2000), 32.

24. Don Cousins, "Laying a Firm Foundation" in "Starting a New Ministry," accessed September 17, 2013, http://www.building churchleaders.com/downloads/practicalministryskills/startinganew ministry/, 46.

Chapter 2

1. Donald McGavran, "How to Grow a Church," 16mm film (Monrovia, Calif.: Church Growth, 1976).

2. Ted Haggard, *Fly Fishing, Dog Training, & Sharing Christ in the 21st Century: Empowering Your Church to Build Community Through Shared Interests* (Nashville: Thomas Nelson, 2002), 11.

3. C. S. Lewis, *The Four Loves* (Orlando: Harcourt Brace, 1988), 247.

4. Stanley Mooneyham in *Who Cares about Love?* by Win Arn, Carroll Nyquist, and Charles Arn (Monrovia, Calif.: Church Growth, 1992), 104.

5. Andy Stanley in "Ga. Megachurch Builds $5M Bridge to Draw the Unchurched" by Lillian Kwon, *Christian Post*, October 15, 2009, http://www.christianpost.com/news/ga-megachurch-builds-5m-bridge-to-draw-the-unchurched-41440/.

6. Thom Turner, "Being Missional = Build a Five Million Dollar Bridge," *Everyday Liturgy*, October 16, 2009, http://every dayliturgy.com/being-missional-build-a-five-million-dollar-bridge/.

7. Rick Warren, "Explosive Growth: Unleash the Creativity of Your Congregation," Rick Warren's Ministry Toolbox #193, March 2, 2005, http://pastors.com.

8. Flavil Ray Yeakley, "Persuasion in Religious Conversion" (Ph.D. dissertation, University of Illinois, 1975), 148.

9. David Stark and Betty Veldman Wieland, *Growing People through Small Groups* (Minneapolis: Bethany, 2004), 94.

Chapter 3

1. Pam Heaton, "Every Church Needs a Profiler," accessed September 18, 2013, http://www.buildingchurchleaders.com/downloads/practicalministryskills/cultivatingactivechurch members/ps07-g.html.

2. Rick Warren, "Explosive Growth: Unleash the Creativity of Your Congregation," Rick Warren's Ministry Toolbox #193, March 2, 2005, http://pastors.com.

Chapter 4

1. Win Arn and Charles Arn, *The Church Growth Ratio Book* (Monrovia, Calif.: Church Growth, 2002), 10.

2. Charles Roesel, "Turn the Church Inside Out" in "Becoming Outward Focused," accessed September 18, 2013, http://www.buildingchurchleaders.com/downloads/training themes/becomingoutwardfocused.

3. Thomas H. Holmes and Richard H. Rahe, "The Social Readjustment Rating Scale," *Journal of Psychosomatic Research* 11, no. 2 (1967): 213–218.

4. Reader comment in Kevin D. Hendricks, "Affinity Churches for Bikers & Cowboys," Church Marketing Sucks, June 28, 2005, http://www.churchmarketingsucks.com/2005/06/affinity-churches-for-bikers-cowboys/.

Chapter 5

1. Mark Howell, "Five Keys to Building a Small Groups Ministry in a Small to Medium-Sized Church," Rick Warren's Ministry Toolbox #145, http://pastors.com.

2. Todd Pridemore, "Does Your Church Have Side Doors?" *Net Results*, September/October 2004, 7.

Chapter 6

1. Alan Nelson, *Me to We: A Pastor's Discovery of the Power of Partnership* (Loveland, Colo.: Group, 2007), 16.

2. Todd Pridemore, "Does Your Church Have Side Doors?" *Net Results*, September/October 2004, 7.

3. Ibid.

4. Pump 'n Praise brochure (Wheaton, Ill.: Wheaton Bible Church).

5. Flavil Ray Yeakley, *Why Churches Grow* (Arvada, Colo.: Christian Communications, 1986), 44.

6. Flavil Ray Yeakley, "Persuasion in Religious Conversion" (Ph.D. dissertation, University of Illinois, 1975), 142.

7. Mark L. Knapp and Anita L. Vangelisti, *Interpersonal Communication and Human Relationships* (Boston: Allyn & Bacon, 2008).

8. Lyle Schaller, "How to Attract New People" in "Cultivating Active Church Members," accessed September 17, 2013, http://www.buildingchurchleaders.com/downloads/practical ministryskills/cultivatingactivechurchmembers/, 3.

Chapter 7

1. "If Only a Map Existed . . . Nazi Mines Stop Egypt's Oil Flow," GIS Development, March 14, 2008, http://www.gis development.net/news/print.asp?id=GIS:N_lifdvcuasz&cat= Industry%20Application&subc=Miscellaneous.

2. Rick Warren, "Explosive Growth: Unleash the Creativity of Your Congregation," Rick Warren's Ministry Toolbox #193, March 2, 2005, http://pastors.com.

3. Lyle Schaller, "How to Attract New People" in "Cultivating Active Church Members," accessed September 17, 2013, http://www.buildingchurchleaders.com/downloads/practical ministryskills/cultivatingactivechurchmembers/, 3.

4. John Moody in "How Externally Focused Churches Minister to Children: The Power of Serving Kids in Your Community" by Krista Petty (Dallas: Leadership Network, 2007), 7.

5. Rev. Dr. John P. Chandler, "3 Minutes," Spence Network, April 16, 2009, http://www.spencenetwork.org/.

6. Harvie Conn and Manuel Ortiz, *Urban Ministry: The Kingdom, the City & the People of God* (Downers Grove, Ill.: InterVarsity Press, 2001), 291.

7. Win Arn, Carroll Nyquist, and Charles Arn, *Who Cares about Love?* (Monrovia, Calif.: Church Growth, 1992), 89–98.

8. Todd Pridemore, "Does Your Church Have Side Doors?" *Net Results*, September/October 2004, 7.

9. George G. Hunter III, *The Apostolic Congregation: Church Growth Reconceived for a New Generation* (Nashville: Abingdon, 2009), 37.

10. Brett Lawrence, "Starbucks Spirituality," *Leadership Journal* (Fall 2002), http://www.christianitytoday.com/le/2002/fall/11.81.html.

11. Nathan Oates, "Growing Christian Community: Through Relational Evangelism and Discipleship" *Vibrant*, Winter, 2008, http://www.vibrantmagazine.org/articles/142-growing-christian-community-through-relational-evangelism-and-discipleship.html.

12. Hunter, *The Apostolic Congregation*, 117.

13. Paul Asay, "Opening Church's Doors First Step to Conversion," *Colorado Springs Gazette*, December 11, 2005, http://gazette.com/opening-churchs-doors-first-step-to-conversion/article/9166.

14. Cecil Maranville, "Flash: Americans Believe in Prayer!" *World News and Prophesy*, January 2004, http://www.ucg.org/christian-living/flash-americans-believe-prayer/.

15. James F. Engel and Wilbert Norton, *What's Gone Wrong With the Harvest? A Communication Strategy for the Church and World Evangelism* (Grand Rapids, Mich.: Zondervan, 1975).

16. Bob Whitesel, *Spiritual Waypoints: Helping Others Navigate the Journey* (Indianapolis: Wesleyan Publishing House), 2010.

17. Charles Arn, "Evangelism or Disciple Making?" *Enrichment Journal*, Spring 2008, 104–110.

18. Rebecca Manley Pippert, interview by Lindy Lowry, "God Came Down: An Interview with Rebecca Manley Pippert," *Outreach Magazine*, March/April 2006, 35.

Chapter 8

1. L. D. Wood-Hull, "A Signature Ministry for St. Barnabas" in *The Messenger* (Portland, Ore.: St. Barnabas Episcopal Church, October 2008).

2. Richard Harris in "Southern Baptist 'Affinity Churches' Tap Niches to Add Members" by Laura Johnston, *Southeast Missourian*, June 18, 2005, http://www.semissourian.com/story/1106160.html.

Epilogue

1. Russell Herman Conwell, "Acres of Diamonds," *Temple University,* public domain, accessed September 19, 2013, http://www.temple.edu/about/history/acres-diamonds.

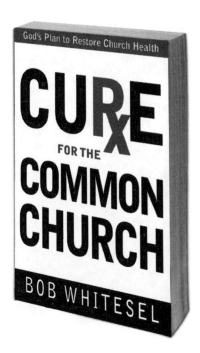

God's answer begins with you. Something is not quite right in the local church. Many Christians see the symptoms of decline in fellowship and spiritual vitality. If health and life are indications of growth, their congregation is not well. Unfortunately, the ailing church is becoming the common church.

Professor and church-growth consultant Bob Whitesel has written *Cure for the Common Church* to offer potent and proven cures to foster health in their local congregations. By thoughtfully examining Scriptures, he applies truths through real-life experience from his years of consulting. Questions for group study also help members explore and discern together how to become a healthy force in their church.

Cure for the Common Church
ISBN: 978-0-89827-587-2

wesleyan
publishing
house

www.wesleyan.org/wph
1.800.493.7539

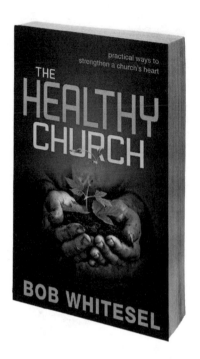

Can an ordinary church become an uncommonly healthy church? Absolutely. But it won't happen automatically. Many average, ordinary churches allow their health to deteriorate to the point that they no longer have the heart to grow strong again. How do some churches fend off this heart deterioration to become uncommonly healthy churches? Professor and church growth consultant Bob Whitesel set out to answer just that question, incorporating two years of research with churches that have not only survived but thrived.

The Healthy Church
ISBN: 978-0-89827-567-4

wesleyan
publishing
house

www.wesleyan.org/wph
1.800.493.7539

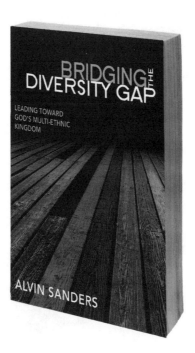

In a diverse, divided world, pastors and church leaders are faced with the question of how to lead across ethnic lines to bring healing and unity to the body of Christ. Author Alvin Sanders believes the church is facing a *chairos* moment—the right time—to address the issue of ethnic division and tension within the church. Through this book, he offers a how-to resource for Christian leaders to lead their organizations in a majority-minority, multi-ethnic America.

Bridging the Diversity Gap
ISBN: 978-0-89827-678-7

wesleyan
publishing
house

www.wesleyan.org/wph
1.800.493.7539

The face of America is growing rapidly more diverse, and many churches are wondering what it means to carry out the Great Commission in a community where different ethnicities are represented. Gary L. McIntosh and Alan McMahan offer a research-based overview of the issues, challenges, and essential principles for developing multi-ethnic churches in the United States. Learn how your church can be effective in welcoming disciples of all ethnicities.

Being the Church in a Multi-Ethnic Community
ISBN: 978-0-89827-490-5

wesleyan
publishing
house

www.wesleyan.org/wph
1.800.493.7539